WHAT YOUR LAWYER DOESN'T WANT YOU TO KNOW

WHAT YOUR LAWYER DOESN'T WANT YOU TO KNOW

Douglas R. Eikermann, JD, LLM

Self-Counsel Press Inc.
(a subsidiary of)
International Self-Counsel Press Ltd.

Printed in Canada.

First edition: 2002

Canadian Cataloguing in Publication Data

Eikermann, Douglas R.
    What your lawyer doesn't want you to know/Douglas R. Eikermann.

    (Self-Counsel legal series)
    ISBN 1-55180-406-9

    1.Attorney and client — United States. I.Title. II. Series.
    KF311.E34 2002   340'.0973   C2002-911097-1

Self-Counsel Press Inc.
(a subsidiary of)
International Self-Counsel Press Ltd.

1704 N. State Street	1481 Charlotte Rd.
Bellingham, WA 98225	North Vancouver, BC V7J 1H1
USA	Canada

ACKNOWLEDGMENTS

I want to thank Catherine Bennett, Michael Bowker, Kathy Huffman Fontenot, Robert G. Frey, Earlene Koons, Caroline Mossie, Rick Schell, and Marty Snyder for reading and critiquing the manuscript.

to Mary Ann

CONTENTS

Samples

INTRODUCTION

Embarking on a journey into the legal world, whether as a party to litigation or as an individual seeking some other form of assistance, is intimidating to most people. As an outsider, you face angry adversaries, strange rules, tough lawyers, and headstrong judges with astonishing authority to make decisions that affect your life. You would like to put your big toe into the legal waters without its being frostbitten, scalded, or severed by something hidden there. With the information contained in this book, you can do just that.

The book is divided into four parts that are further subdivided into chapters, eight in all. Part I presents a series of steps that will help you choose the right lawyer. The process requires some attention to detail, but if you follow it carefully, you will dramatically improve your chances of finding a lawyer suited to your legal problem, your personality, and your pocketbook. This first portion of the book also contains sections that deal with aspects of searching for and using lawyers who practice in specific areas of law — general practice, criminal defense, divorce, personal injury, real estate, and traffic court. These areas merit special comment because they are of interest to a broad spectrum of readers. The remainder of Part I is about negotiating and executing an attorney-client agreement. If your relationship with your lawyer is clearly defined in writing, you will avoid many of the perils that too frequently befall the uninitiated as they make their precarious ways through the legal jungle.

Part II explains how to manage your lawyer once you have chosen one. Even a mediocre lawyer, when managed properly, can in most situations do an acceptable job. Run-of-the-mill lawyers frequently obtain good results for their clients. If the lawyer you select happens to be a superior one, however, and you are a good manager as well, excellent results can be forthcoming.

Part III sets forth what you should do if you have a serious problem with your lawyer. Poor performance on a case, legal malpractice, and unethical activities all harm you, but the remedies for them are different. What you do to resolve a conflict with your lawyer will vary depending on the category into which the conflict falls. This section provides you with an overview of the performance and ethical standards that you can expect from your lawyer and directs you on how to proceed if your lawyer's conduct falls short of meeting those standards.

Part IV deals with arbitration, mediation, and small claims court. Collectively, these options are referred to as Alternative Dispute Resolution (ADR), and they function as alternatives to normal litigation that are available in specific situations.

This book is not designed to guide you in the prosecution of a case without a lawyer. In fact, you will find almost no law in the book at all. If the legal matter you are facing is one in which your health, liberty, or assets are at stake, you need the assistance of a professional who knows the rules. Should you choose to enter the legal fray on your own, you will not likely achieve a result equal to that which a lawyer would obtain. This book is intended to help you find the right lawyer and manage that lawyer's efforts on your behalf. If you wish to inform yourself in broad terms about the legal process, and you want to learn how to hire and manage a lawyer, this book is for you. If you seek detailed instructions for representing yourself in court, it is not.

Each state has its own laws and procedures, and I do not pretend to know them all. Reading this book will give you a feel for the difficulties that you will encounter in most jurisdictions and provide you with suggestions for overcoming them. No suggestion made, however, should override your own good judgment in meeting a specific challenge. If you become actively involved in your case, and you use common sense, you will find good solutions to most of the problems that confront you. Common sense, though, is always based on some knowledge, and the essential information that you need to hire, manage, and fire a lawyer is contained in these pages.

PART I

FINDING A LAWYER AND GETTING STARTED

CHAPTER 1

SELECTING A LAWYER

Some folks live happily and die peacefully without ever entering a lawyer's office. Others may need a lawyer only once, perhaps to draft a will or probate the estate of a deceased relative. You probably have family members or friends who have never seen the inside of a courtroom as litigants, perhaps having only appeared there occasionally for jury service. When I was growing up, my parents did not personally know any lawyers to whom they could turn for guidance with respect to legal matters. Individuals have few opportunities to practice choosing lawyers, and once they have had occasion to select the first one, frequently no subsequent chance presents itself to apply the knowledge they have gained.

The attributes of a good lawyer are a mystery to most non-lawyers. People are generally aware that not all lawyers are good ones, but notions among laypersons regarding the specific characteristics that a good lawyer possesses are usually vague. Recommendations from friends and acquaintances are often based on reports regarding a lawyer's performance on a specific case rather than on any objective criteria. In order to select the right lawyer for your situation, you need a methodology that allows you to identify specific qualities that the lawyer must have in order to be acceptable to you. This chapter presents such a methodology. Here, you will find the basic information you need, not to perform your own legal work, but rather to select the appropriate lawyer to do the work for you.

Although the legal approach may vary from case to case, the process you should use to select a lawyer is the same whether you want to draft a will, negotiate a contract, or prosecute a lawsuit. It consists of determining whether or not you need a lawyer, then selecting one by gathering information and answering a series of questions. If you diligently follow this discipline, you will maximize your chances of finding a lawyer who fits your case, personality, and bank account.

If you are litigation bound, you have three choices. First, you can represent yourself. This is called *pro se*[1] representation. You always have a right to do your own legal work, whether in court or out. It is not, however, wise to do so in most instances. Second, you may, in some situations, submit the matter to one of several forms of Alternative Dispute Resolution (ADR). ADR is a general term for the resolution of disputes in forums outside of the public court system. If your case is a litigation matter appropriate for arbitration or mediation, one of those methods might work for you. Third, you can employ a lawyer to take your case through the public court system. If the legal problem you face is one in which representing yourself would be unwise and ADR would be inappropriate, you must select a lawyer who can guide your case through court and help you deal with the jumble of problems that will confront you along the way.

1. Do You Really Need a Lawyer?

You always have the right to represent yourself in court. In lower courts, such as traffic court or small claims court, *pro se* representation is commonplace. But if your case is one with much at stake, and the rules allow you to have a lawyer, representing yourself is almost always a bad idea.

---

1. The term varies with the jurisdiction. *Pro se* is the most common, but *in propria persona*, *pro persona*, and *pro per* are used as well.

Most judges dread the appearance of a self-represented party in their courtrooms. They generally consider it an inconvenience to have to explain basic rules to a bumbling nonlawyer who does not understand the procedures, concepts, terminology, or courtesies that surround the proceedings. Frequently, a judge will commence a hearing[2] or a trial with a sincere desire to accommodate the person who appears without a lawyer, but patience soon wears thin, and what at first looks like an advantage for the individual usually becomes a handicap.

The same thing happens before a jury. The party appearing alone may gain some initial sympathy from the jurors and actually function fairly well at trial for a few minutes or even several hours. But as the day drags on the mistakes compound, and even the most forgiving of jurors becomes disenchanted. The opposing lawyer, if reasonably cunning, will wait patiently for the *pro se* party to self-destruct. The lawyer will look like a picture of reasonableness and competence compared to the graceless individual who is trying to exercise the right to self-representation. It is extremely difficult to complete a hearing or trial as a nonlawyer and come out looking sane.

Another problem with representing yourself is that it may harm your case if you change your mind and hire a lawyer in midstream. Almost all of the posturing for a trial takes place beforehand. Representing yourself in the early stages of your case with the intention of turning it over to a lawyer who will take it to trial is not sound litigation strategy. Many lawyers refuse to take such cases, but if one were to accept yours, you would probably forfeit any claim against that lawyer for malpractice should something go awry.

Typically, individuals who represent themselves in civil lawsuits[3] do not save money. A good lawyer, managed properly, will normally achieve a monetary outcome that is superior to any you might obtain on your own. Frequently, the difference will be more than enough to cover the lawyer's compensation. Consider

---

2. A hearing is a court session before a judge that is not a formal trial.

3. A civil lawsuit deals with private rights and remedies that are noncriminal. A criminal action, by contrast, is one brought by the government to punish offenses against the public.

it an investment. If you select the appropriate lawyer for your case and effectively manage that lawyer's activities, you will get the most value for your dollar.

You can save money by performing selected tasks for your lawyer. If, for instance, the opposition requests that you produce documents, you can help by identifying the documents, putting them in order, and delivering them to your lawyer's office, perhaps even with a second copy. (Be sure to keep photocopies for your own records as well.) The fees skyrocket when the lawyer, an associate lawyer, or a paralegal assistant must leave the law office to sort through a client's files.

Other ways to save money include obtaining photocopies of public documents, searching public records, compiling data, and taking photographs. You can save hundreds and sometimes thousands of dollars by helping with this routine investigative work. An added advantage to participating in these activities is that you become directly involved in your case. If you provide information to your lawyer quickly, perhaps you can then expect that your matter will receive some added personal attention. Lawyers take more interest in clients who show concern about their situations.

If you insist, however, on representing yourself in court, you should consult with a lawyer beforehand to help you avoid making serious errors. It would be wise to pay for a few hours of coaching on the law applicable to your case and on courtroom procedure. You may conclude, after the consultation, that the lawyer has a valuable service to offer you and that using that service is more prudent than struggling through the details on your own.

2. Six Steps to Shopping for a Lawyer

Your search for the right lawyer does not have to be haphazard. The selection method set out in this section is based on personal interviews with lawyers. If you faithfully follow this approach, you will substantially increase your chances of finding the right lawyer for your situation.

No one can do your lawyer shopping for you. Only you can decide which lawyer is right for your personality and for the problem you want to solve. A lawyer's credentials may fulfill all of the objective criteria for your case, but your personalities may clash. If you do not feel comfortable with one lawyer, look for another. Lawyers are plentiful. If you persevere in your search, you will find one who fits your needs.

Below are six steps that you should diligently take to select a lawyer. The explanation of the steps is followed by a series of short descriptions of selected areas of law practice. The descriptions are meant to introduce you to some of the types of lawyers available and, considered in conjunction with the six steps, will help you find the lawyer who is right for your situation.

2.1 Identifying your legal problem

Your first step in finding a lawyer is to identify the nature of the legal problem you want to solve. For instance, if you want a divorce, it makes sense to seek a divorce lawyer. If creditors are pursuing you, however, you do not need a divorce lawyer but rather one who knows about debtor's rights.

In some instances, you may find it difficult to identify the legal category into which your problem falls. Making a couple of simple telephone calls will help you with this dilemma, and doing so should incur no legal fees. Just call a lawyer or two and briefly relate your story. Most lawyers will, without much fanfare, tell you what kind of law they practice and what kind of legal expertise your problem requires. After talking to a couple of them, you will almost certainly know the appropriate area of law for your search. In most instances, a single conversation will be sufficient to give you enough information regarding the nature of the problem and the kind of lawyer you should seek.

It is possible to be fooled, though, so you'll want to be on your toes when you make these initial calls. Some lawyers do not have the quantity or quality of cases that they would like to have. If your case is potentially lucrative, lawyers whose areas of emphasis are unrelated to the one required for your situation may try to convince you to sign up with them. If you have been involved in an accident, for instance, and have a high-dollar personal injury matter to pursue, even a lawyer with little trial experience may claim to do personal injury law. Your strict attention to the other five steps outlined below, however, will allow you to identify the qualified lawyers and select the one who is best for you.

2.2 Making a list of candidates

The next step is to compile a list of lawyers whom you will interview before you select the one you want. Taking a friend's recommendation on blind faith, walking through the door of the first law office you come to, or choosing a name at random from the telephone book are not advisable methods for making your selection. Lots of bad lawyers advertise in the telephone book. Big, expensive advertisements are no indication that a lawyer is competent or ethical.

Referrals from referral services and most referrals by lawyers carry built-in biases. The best lawyers are busy and often do not take referrals from referral services, so that avenue may not generate the best list of prospects. Also, lawyers who refer cases to colleagues frequently have fee-splitting agreements with them or expect to receive referrals in return. Such a lawyer may shuffle you off to the lawyer who has promised the best deal rather than the one who is best qualified to work on your case.

For these and other reasons, you should interview several lawyers and compare approaches, personalities, and fees. Once you've considered all options, you will be prepared to make a rational choice. You can draw from a number of sources to generate an initial list of prospects. No single source is better than another; you should consider all of them in making your list. Some of those sources are —

- recommendations from business acquaintances, professionals, relatives, or friends. Such recommendations should be supported by specific reasons why the lawyer would be appropriate for your case.

- referrals from local and state bar associations, legal aid organizations, public interest groups, law schools, lawyer referral services, and private legal clinics.

- the Yellow Pages, directories, Martindale-Hubbell (a well-known directory of lawyers), Internet Web sites, and other written referral sources. Often, lawyers will place themselves in such directories under the area of law that interests them. In some states, lawyers must pass a rigorous examination to be allowed to advertise as specialists. In others, they are prohibited from holding themselves forth as such. Just because a lawyer is listed under the area of law that applies to your situation, however, does not necessarily mean that it is advisable to choose that lawyer. At this point, you are simply making a list of candidates from which you will later select the person who will handle your case.

2.3 Setting up the interviews

Once you have constructed a list of four or five lawyers, you should telephone each one and ask several brief questions. If you can, limit this first conversation to three basic areas of inquiry:

- Does the lawyer practice in the area of law that your case requires?

- Is there a fee for an initial consultation?

- Can you make an appointment?

Try to avoid doing a full-fledged interview over the telephone. If you correctly follow the six steps outlined in this chapter, a telephone call alone is not sufficient to make your final selection. You will learn far more by interviewing each lawyer in person. You should use the telephone only for the preliminary screening. Wait until the interview to discuss the details of your case. The first telephone call is just to make sure that the lawyer does the kind of work that your case requires and to make an appointment.

You should ask beforehand whether the lawyer charges for initial consultations. If you wait until you have received what might be construed as legal advice, it may be too late to avoid paying a fee. Most lawyers will not charge you for the telephone call or your first meeting. Just ask if there is a fee for the initial consultation, and if there is, politely end the conversation and call another lawyer. (If your legal situation is unique, however, and a lawyer with expertise in a specific area of law indicates that there will be a fee for an initial consultation, you may want to see that lawyer and pay the fee. I know of one exceptional circumstance in which a Japanese businessman paid $1,000 to an immigration lawyer for a consultation on a Sunday afternoon. The consultation lasted about two hours, and both lawyer and client left the meeting feeling pleased with the outcome.)

Once you have telephoned each of the lawyers, review your notes and narrow your list to three. You should be able to eliminate one or two lawyers based on your first impressions. You can come back to them later should your remaining options fail to produce the lawyer you want, but for the moment, you should cancel the appointments with the ones you have decided not to interview. You will attempt to make your selection from the three lawyers who remain on your list. If, however, after the interviews you decide that none of these lawyers suits your needs, you can make an appointment with one or more of the discarded ones, or simply start over and generate an entirely new list.

2.4 Preparing for the interviews

You should prepare for the interviews by making a list of facts surrounding your case, and then a list of questions regarding the lawyer's approach to the case and relationship with you. Make each list separately and leave enough space between items for you to take notes as you interview the prospective lawyer. To construct your list of facts, write down every relevant thing you can remember. You may want to carry the list with you for a few days so that you can add to it whenever a new thought comes to mind.

2.5 Conducting the interviews

The purpose of an interview is to garner just enough information to decide whether or not you want to place your case with that lawyer. It is not a time for seeking full-fledged advice on your legal problem, although you may find that difficult to resist. Some of the questions you ask may naturally lead to a discussion of the whole matter. The order in which you pose your questions is not too important; just make sure you cover all of the important areas before you leave. At each interview, you should —

- ascertain the experience level of the lawyer,
- understand in general terms the legal approach that will be taken in your case,
- learn what services the lawyer will perform,
- inquire about the fee to be charged for those services, and
- determine whether you can work comfortably with the lawyer.

To accomplish these things, you may also want to ask some or all of the following questions, along with any others that may occur to you:

- How long have you practiced law? (You cannot assume that a 50-year-old lawyer is experienced. Although most lawyers graduate from law school early in life, each graduating class includes some older students.)
- How long have you practiced in this jurisdiction?
- What is your relationship with the judge? (You may not get very far with this question. After all, what lawyer would tell a client about a relationship with a judge that might affect the outcome of a case? You should ask the question anyway, though, because it lets the lawyer know that you are thinking about all aspects of the legal system.)
- Into what category of law does my case fall?
- What are my legal options?
- How many cases of this type have you done?
- What approach would you take to my case?
- What will be the probable result of my case?
- How long will it take to bring the case to a conclusion?
- What fee arrangement do you propose?
- Do you require a deposit?

- Do you use a written fee agreement or engagement letter?
- How much do you expect the total legal fees and expenses to be in my case?
- Do you have malpractice insurance coverage?
- What is the name of the insurance company?
- Have any disciplinary complaints been filed against you?
- What were the bases for those complaints?

You'll have to tailor the questions to your situation. Common sense should be your guide. If the lawyer is 27 years old, there's no point to asking the question regarding years of practice. You would, however, want to ask how many similar cases the lawyer has handled.

If you are seeking a lawyer to defend you, you should also try to learn at the interview what relationship your lawyer has with the opposing lawyer. That relationship is especially important in small communities where a few lawyers face each other repeatedly. You may want to ask some of the following questions:

- How well do you know my opponent's lawyer?
- Have you tried any cases against one another?
- Have you referred cases to one another? Were referral fees paid?
- Are there any hostile feelings or scores to settle between you that might affect your judgment in my case?

As the interviews progress, you will find each one to be easier than the last. Your knowledge of your case, the lawyers' personalities, the services at your disposal, and the fee structures will increase rapidly, and you will feel a growing confidence that your final choice will be a good one. Do not skip any of the steps outlined here. If you are meticulous, you will make a good selection and gain momentum that will help you throughout your case.

The only good way to compare lawyers is to meet each one face to face. During the interview, you should observe other aspects of the lawyer's business operation as well, such as the general appearance of the office and the attitudes of the employees.

The interview is a two-way street. You, the potential client, are also being interviewed and evaluated by the lawyer. No lawyer has to accept your case, so you will want to make a positive impression. Good lawyers look for clients who will work with them as a team. If you take a professional approach to the interview, you will obtain the information about the lawyer that you seek and at the same time demonstrate that you are a desirable future client.

2.6 Making the final selection

Your diligence and hard work in comparing lawyers will pay off. After speaking with several of them about your case, you will know much more about —

- the range of services available;
- the range of fees charged and the different methods of payment;
- the possible approaches to your legal problem;
- the personalities of the lawyers; and
- the ages, reputations, and experience levels of the lawyers.

You should meet with at least three lawyers before you make your selection. Do not sign an attorney-client agreement until you have talked to all of them. Some lawyers may encourage you to sign up with their firms at the interview. Be strong. Resist the temptation to contract with any of them until you are sure that you know all your options. You will have an urge to make a quick decision and to turn your worries over to the first reasonable lawyer you encounter. That impulse is normal, but you should resist it. Take your time and do each interview thoroughly.[4]

After the interviews, review your notes and draw comparisons. Then ask yourself which lawyer you feel you can work with the best. After undertaking this evaluation process, the right choice should be obvious. If you still do not know which one to choose, you may have to repeat this six-step process until you are satisfied. In all probability, though, your preference will be clear, and you will be ready to move to the next step: defining the

4. While taking your time is important, you must use common sense. Do not take so much time that you let statutes of limitations run out.

precise relationship you will have with your lawyer through the drafting and execution of an attorney-client agreement. Details about attorney-client agreements appear in Chapter 2.

3. Some Specific Areas of the Law

When you choose a lawyer, you should follow the steps outlined above. Before you go through that process, however, you will find it useful to read about some of the areas of law in which lawyers engage. Such general knowledge will give you added self-confidence as you conduct your interviews, even if it does not relate directly to your case.

The following six subsections contain information about lawyers who operate in the general practice, criminal defense, divorce, personal injury, real estate, and traffic court arenas. The descriptions are far from exhaustive in their treatment of these areas of law; entire volumes have been published on each topic. Other important topics are omitted entirely. These six areas are included here because they are the ones about which most readers will want to know. Even if your legal problem does not fit neatly into one of them, the explanations will be useful to orient you to what lawyers do. The information will give you additional insight into the practice of law and assist you in finding a good lawyer.

3.1 General practice lawyers

The old-fashioned general practitioner, the maverick jack-of-all-trades lawyer who did a middling bit of legal work for everyone in the community, is a dying breed. The role of these lawyers was not unlike that of the erstwhile family physician who made house calls and served as a general problem solver for the community. The traditional generalist handled divorces, criminal defenses, real estate closings, property disputes, contract negotiations, personal injury lawsuits, worker's compensation claims, adoptions, bankruptcies, estate planning matters, probate cases, and more. These days, a lawyer who attempts to practice in such a broad range of areas runs a high risk of committing legal malpractice. The practice of law has become so complicated that most lawyers can claim competence in only one or two areas.

In the United States, the ratio of practicing lawyers to consumers exceeds that of most other countries. The competition among lawyers is stiff. When a lawyer lacks work and the overhead monster rears its ugly head, the temptation to accept any client who walks through the door is strong. Few lawyers turn down cases that fall outside of their areas of expertise when pushed to pay the rent and the secretary's salary.

The client-consumer is the unfortunate victim of this tendency. No lawyer can know enough to process all of the cases that may present themselves. In modern-day firms, lawyers shift cases back and forth among themselves according to expertise and interest. Lawyers in small firms often work together as a team, with one of them accepting family-related matters, another handling criminal cases, a third taking business clients, and yet another doing the personal injury work. The family, criminal, and business lawyers establish a broad client base for the firm while allowing the personal injury lawyer to concentrate on the big-money cases.

The individual general practitioner is probably a figure of historical note only. The risk of committing errors is great for lawyers who do a little of everything. The concept of a general law practice lives on, however, in the absence of its central figure, the general practitioner. Groups of lawyers who know their limitations and who wisely allocate cases among themselves according to area of emphasis, level of experience, and personal preference now offer the broad range of services that once was the province of the general practitioner.

3.2   Criminal-defense lawyers

For criminal matters, you need a lawyer whose practice focuses on criminal law and who knows the judges, prosecutors, probation officers, bailiffs, clerks, and courthouse secretaries. Much of criminal-law practice involves bargaining with the prosecution. Experienced criminal-defense lawyers know what options are available, which prosecutors tend to cut the best deals, and how each judge will respond to the agreed-upon terms.

Some prosecutors won't plea bargain, but most will. Be aware, however, that they enter into plea agreements not because they are nice guys or sympathetic people, but rather because in most jurisdictions there are so many criminal cases that they cannot possibly take them all to trial. Prosecutors usually dismiss the cases that are hard to prove and plea bargain on most of the others. This practice allows them to concentrate their efforts on the preparation of high-profile cases.

In some jurisdictions, all practicing lawyers must accept court-appointed criminal cases. Judges appoint lawyers to defend accused persons in criminal cases when the individuals cannot afford to pay for representation. Here are some observations regarding court-appointed lawyers:

- Lawyers in need of work or trial experience often seek court appointments.
- Court-appointed lawyers sometimes go to great lengths to avoid taking their cases to trial, perhaps reassigning them to associate lawyers or hastily recommending guilty pleas.
- Lawyers who do not practice criminal law but who are nevertheless appointed to defend indigent defendants may have scanty knowledge of criminal-defense practice, perhaps little more than what they remember from their criminal-law and procedure courses in law school. Although they may be fine professionals in their principal areas of practice, they may not be competent in handling criminal matters.
- Court-appointed lawyers are paid relatively low hourly fees. In addition, many jurisdictions place a maximum on the overall amount that can be charged per appointment. Such limitations on lawyers' compensation act as disincentives: lawyers are less likely to search for creative ways to defend their clients.

The goal of a good criminal lawyer in defending an accused person is not necessarily to help the individual escape punishment, although every criminal-defense lawyer derives pleasure from obtaining a verdict of not guilty. Of course, if the defendant is truly innocent, obtaining that person's freedom should always be the lawyer's objective. Only rarely, though, is the accused wholly innocent of wrongdoing. Usually, the person has engaged in some questionable, immature, or unwise act and is charged with that and any other related offenses that zealous prosecutors find by searching through the Penal Code. One important job of the criminal-defense lawyer is to ensure that the charges brought against the defendant are consistent with the facts of the case. The lawyer also ensures that each pretrial step and the trial itself are executed fairly and in accordance with the protections set forth in the United States Constitution.

3.3 Divorce lawyers

Some divorce clients attempt to use their lawyers as psychologists or counselors. You should not choose a divorce lawyer by selecting the most empathetic or sympathetic individual from your list of candidates. If you are distressed by your separation from your spouse and want emotional support, you should seek the help of a professional counselor, psychologist, or psychiatrist. If you want your side of your divorce case presented clearly and effectively, and your interests protected under the law, find a good divorce lawyer. Some of the toughest and most knowledgeable lawyers in the legal profession are divorce lawyers. They are a breed all their own, but perhaps just what you need to get the job done.

For people without the resources to pay normal legal fees, most jurisdictions have public-service organizations that handle divorce cases for moderate sums. These lawyers do a reasonably good job, but they usually have heavy caseloads, and access to their services is contingent on qualifying under stringent rules.

Here are some things to consider in your selection of a divorce lawyer:

- Does the lawyer primarily operate a family-law[5] practice? Divorce law is becoming more demanding every day. You should seek a lawyer whose law practice consists of a substantial number of divorce and child-custody matters. Most jurisdictions have local rules surrounding divorce — special judges, appointed magistrates, mandatory mediation,

---

5. Family law includes divorce, adoption, child custody, and more.

obligatory counseling for parents — and it's important that your lawyer be familiar with all of the requirements. At the initial interview, ask what percentage of the lawyer's practice is made up of divorce cases. If the figure is low, you may want to seek another lawyer.

- Is the fee hourly or fixed? Beware of fixed-fee divorces unless you are absolutely certain that there will be no contested issues. Lawyers who do divorces for a fixed fee rely on volume to make money. Paralegal assistants and secretaries may handle most of the paperwork for your case. These people are usually qualified to do repetitive tasks, but they are unlikely to notice details requiring special attention in a specific matter. That's your lawyer's job.

If you pay a fixed fee based on your expectation that your divorce will be uncontested, and along the way your spouse decides to dispute something, your lawyer is likely to ask you for more money. You may end up paying just as much as you would have had you retained a lawyer on an hourly basis. Listen carefully during the initial interview. The lawyer will probably warn you that if any issue becomes contested, the fixed-fee arrangement will automatically switch to an hourly one.[6] At that point, you may be obligated to make an additional deposit before the lawyer will continue working on your case.

Divorces are commonly done for hourly fees, with a retainer[7] of $500 to $10,000 or more to start the case. The money is deposited into the lawyer's trust account, and the lawyer bills against it for the hours worked. Once the initial retainer is exhausted, the lawyer bills the client monthly thereafter. Some lawyers ask for additional retainers each time the prior one is gone. You should reach a clear understanding regarding such fee matters before the case begins, and the details should be included in the fee agreement. Also, if you are to be billed on an hourly

---

6. If this condition is not communicated verbally, it may appear as a seemingly innocuous paragraph in the fee agreement.

7. Some minor confusion surrounds the use of the word "retainer." Here it refers to a deposit that the lawyer takes before starting to work on a case and is sometimes called a "special retainer." The term may also be used, however, to refer to a set monthly fee that a lawyer receives from a client to remain on call for any legal matter that might arise. This fee is sometimes called a "general retainer" and is discussed in greater detail in Chapter 2.

basis, you should not agree to forfeit the retainer in the event the case settles or you change lawyers. The lawyer should take only the fees for work done to the point of disengagement and return the remaining money to you. Fee agreements are covered in Chapter 2.

- Will you need a temporary restraining order or an injunction to protect you from threats, annoying phone calls, physical abuse, and other intrusive acts by your estranged spouse? If your lawyer hesitates to employ those remedies, and you sincerely feel they are necessary, you should insist that the lawyer seek them for you.

- Is your spouse preparing to file for divorce? If you suspect that your spouse is seriously contemplating divorce, you should consider being the first to file. The initiating party gains some important legal and psychological advantages in the case, and you may strengthen your bargaining position greatly by getting off the starting line first. Do not procrastinate. See a lawyer early to find out if waiting will prejudice your case.

Another reason to hire a lawyer promptly is that many smaller communities have only one tough divorce lawyer or one law firm with a good reputation in the family law area. If you are the first to retain that lawyer or firm, your spouse will have to go elsewhere. To accomplish this, you need not file for divorce right away. Just establish the attorney-client relationship so that your spouse will be precluded from using that firm.

3.4 *Personal injury lawyers*

A personal injury case is one in which a person claims to have been harmed as a result of someone's intentional, reckless, or negligent act. Often these cases have the potential for recoveries of large sums of money. If you have suffered a severe injury, you may find that every lawyer with whom you talk wants to represent you. You should not, however, become sidetracked just because a lawyer wants your case. You should proceed with the steps outlined in the first part of this chapter and make your selection based on the factors set forth there.

If your case is one in which damages[8] are potentially large, you need a lawyer who does personal injury work on a regular basis, has a track record of success, and has a reputation for skill in the courtroom. Your lawyer's reputation for prowess in court is extremely important. In one case, an insurance company extended a $300,000 settlement[9] offer to an injured man whose case was being handled by a lawyer who did mostly business-related legal work and had not spent much time in the courtroom. The lawyer, seeing a nice chunk of change on the table for little effort, recommended settlement. The client became suspicious, fired the lawyer, and employed one whose practice emphasized personal injury litigation and who had a reputation for doing well at trial. With the new lawyer working on the matter, the offer climbed steadily during the subsequent months, and the case finally settled for $850,000 a few days before trial.

Any lawyer could have "won" a settlement of $300,000 in that case. But a skilled lawyer with a good reputation was able to squeeze the defendant (in this case, backed by an insurance company) for nearly three times that amount. The personal injury lawyer was clearly worth the fee he took from the settlement. Both lawyers had contracts with the client that contained contingency fee provisions of one-third of the net proceeds. With the help of a skilled trial lawyer, though, the client took home $566,667 instead of $200,000.[10]

Settlements are based on what the opposing parties and lawyers believe will happen at trial. If your lawyer is young and has not established a reputation, such a prediction becomes difficult, and the settlement value of your case may be much lower than it would be were it placed with a lawyer known for convincing juries to award large sums of money. A defense lawyer may not feel compelled to make an attractive settlement offer to a lawyer with no reputation for winning in court. In addition, an experienced lawyer will do better at trial if the case does not settle. At trial, too, the age of the lawyer can be a factor. A lawyer with a few gray hairs may be more likely to win the respect and favor

---

8. Damages are money claimed by a person as compensation for an injury or loss.

9. A settlement is an agreement between the parties to end a dispute or lawsuit.

10. For the purpose of this illustration, these figures are calculated without taking expenses into account.

of a jury than one a bit younger. You should seek a lawyer with the poise, believability, and charisma to attract jurors' votes.

When you first meet with your personal injury lawyer, you will receive an attorney-client agreement establishing the relationship and the fee arrangement for the case. Normally it will be a contingency-fee contract, which means that the lawyer is paid a percentage of the amount recovered in the matter. The contingency arrangement may provide for a fee as a percentage of the net proceeds, such as 33$\frac{1}{3}$ percent of the recovery[11] after all expenses have been paid. Or it may be graduated, with possible fees ranging from 25 percent to 40 percent, depending on the time of settlement or disposition of the case at trial or on appeal. A contingency fee of 50 percent or more may be appropriate on collection cases or under other special circumstances. Contingency fees are explained in detail in Chapter 2.

You should insist that the contingency fee be calculated based on the net proceeds from the recovery. Many lawyers will resist this and will want to calculate the fees from the gross proceeds or to include a clause in the fee agreement to protect themselves if the expenses are greater than the recovery. In some states, though, lawyers are required to calculate their fees from the net proceeds. The net proceeds are the portion of the recovery that remains after deducting expenses such as expert witness fees, deposition[12] charges, travel, filing fees, and the costs of special exhibits for trial. Ask your lawyer to define net proceeds in the attorney-client agreement, and when the case is over, you should request a statement that sets forth all expenses in detail.

You should also request periodic expense reports as your case moves toward trial. In many jurisdictions, the client must pay the expenses even if there is no recovery at the end of the case, so it's important always to know where you stand. Some lawyers will try to get you to agree to pay part or all of the expenses as they become due. This may or may not be a reasonable request, depending on the situation, and if your lawyer insists upon it, you will certainly want to compare the suggested approach with that

---

11. A recovery is an amount of money awarded in or collected from a judgment or settlement.

12. A deposition is out-of-court testimony of a witness that is put into booklet form by a court reporter and used in court or for information gathering.

of other lawyers in the same jurisdiction. Expenses are discussed further in Chapter 2.

You should try to construct the fee agreement as a joint business venture between you and your lawyer. Your lawyer's willingness to invest time and money in your case is an indication that it has value. You must be careful, however, to follow the case closely, because excessive costs can also cause a cold-footed lawyer to recommend settling prematurely. In some instances, it may be desirable to ascertain beforehand whether the law firm has enough money to proceed to the end of the case. It is not uncommon for a law firm to invest thousands of dollars of its own money in a meritorious personal injury case.

An insistence on your part that the law firm front expenses accomplishes two important goals for you. First, as a true partner with real money (not just time) invested in your case, your lawyer will give your case high priority. If the lawyer's money is involved, you can rest assured that your legal problem will not be ignored. Your lawyer will want to recover the investment, with a profit, as soon as possible, and thus will be more likely to push your case to a conclusion.

Second, a lawyer's willingness to invest in your case is an excellent indicator of the strength of your legal position. If you shop around and find that no lawyer will represent you unless you make a deposit for expenses, you may want to refrain from taking legal action. Lawyers are like other investors: if there is money to be made, they may gamble; but if the risk is too high or the reward too small, they may refuse to take a chance. Such a refusal is a red flag indicating that your case may not be a strong one. Be sure to consult with several lawyers, however, before you come to such a conclusion. In most scenarios, you will eventually pay the expenses because they will be taken from the recovery, but while the case is pending, your lawyer should be willing to provide those funds.

3.5 Real estate lawyers

In most jurisdictions, you will find a few lawyers who concentrate their efforts on real estate matters. Title insurance companies sometimes hire lawyers to prepare closing documents for their customers for a modest fixed fee. Some states require that a lawyer draft the documents that a title company uses at a real estate closing even if neither the buyer nor the seller desires legal representation.

Many large law firms have real estate law departments. For run-of-the-mill residential closings, however, their fees may be prohibitive, and unless some special twist is involved, employing a high-priced lawyer to review routine residential closings is overkill. The title-insurance policy covers most contingencies, but you may want to have a lawyer review the exceptions that are cited in the title commitment. For commercial real estate matters, the real estate department of a larger firm may have the collective experience and expertise necessary to coordinate the various aspects of complicated deals. Mid-size law firms may also have rather impressive real estate departments, so some lawyer shopping is in order. You should not assume, however, that because a law firm is large or because its real estate department has a good reputation, the individual lawyer assigned to you is necessarily a good one. You should go through the same process for choosing a lawyer that was introduced at the beginning of this chapter, interviewing several of them before you make your final selection.

Fees for work on residential real estate transactions are often fixed and sometimes can be quite reasonable, but for the larger commercial deals, the lawyer will usually propose some other method for calculating them. Beware of percentage fee arrangements on real estate transactions: such schemes frequently produce windfall earnings for lawyers. Whatever the fee structure, you should strive for an arrangement that provides for a rational relationship between the work to be performed and the compensation proposed.

The seller's lawyer does the bulk of the legal work in a residential closing, preparing the deeds, deeds of trust, assumption papers, promissory notes, and other documents needed by the parties to the transaction. A few days before the closing date, the seller's lawyer sends copies of the closing statement and all supporting documents to the buyer's lawyer for review and comment. The buyer's lawyer then checks the documents and points out any problems. If you are a buyer in a residential real estate transaction, review your lawyer's fee statement carefully to see what your lawyer did for the fee. In days gone by, when the buyer's lawyer performed a title search to certify clear title, the buyer's lawyer had more work to do and accepted some rather substantial professional risk. With title insurance now the rule rather than the exception, however, the role of the buyer's lawyer has diminished.

Nonetheless, you, as a buyer, should not try to close a deal without a lawyer. Only sophisticated buyers should attempt to close without a lawyer's reviewing the closing documents beforehand. Even if the seller purchases title insurance, and a lawyer for the seller or a lawyer selected by the title-insurance company drafts the documents, you should have your own lawyer review that work to ensure nothing is overlooked. Such a review should not cost very much, and your security and peace of mind are worth the expense.

If a title-insurance company performs the closing, and a lawyer drafts the closing documents, that lawyer normally will not prepare the closing statement. You should make sure that you understand exactly which documents the title-insurance company's closer will prepare and which ones will be the lawyer's responsibility. The lawyer does not calculate the money amounts that are to be inserted into the promissory note and other documents, but simply copies into the note the numbers provided by the title-insurance company, the broker, or the parties. If the amounts are incorrect, the lawyer may not be responsible. You should make certain that the closing statement correctly reflects the transaction as set forth in the purchase agreement. Of course, your broker and the title-insurance company's closer should calculate the amounts correctly, but people make mistakes, and it makes good sense to ensure that the lawyer receives accurate information.

If your real estate problem consists of a court action involving real property,[13] you need a trial lawyer who is familiar with

---

13. Real property is property that is permanent, fixed, and immovable (i.e., land).

such questions. A real estate office practice differs from a real estate litigation practice. Many transactional real estate lawyers never see the inside of a courtroom. For real estate litigation, ideally you should employ a trial lawyer who has litigated real estate issues. If, however, you are forced to choose between a trial lawyer with no real estate background and a real estate lawyer with no trial experience, you should choose the trial lawyer. A good trial lawyer can learn the real estate principles applicable to a particular situation and do a competent job, but a real estate lawyer cannot learn to be a trial lawyer while preparing for one case.

3.6 Traffic court lawyers

Every jurisdiction has several lawyers who spend nearly all their time in traffic court. Most of us would go crazy doing such repetitive work, but these lawyers have refined the practice into a science and usually obtain better results at lower prices than lawyers who appear in traffic court only occasionally.

Sometimes they process cases without ever speaking directly to the client. A secretary may take the information regarding the offense, ask for payment of a fixed fee (usually surprisingly low if the violation does not involve repeated offenses, alcohol, drugs, or other complications), and tell you to wait until someone from the law office calls you. The rules vary from jurisdiction to jurisdiction, but often the next thing you will receive is a phone call from the secretary or a letter from the lawyer informing you that your case has been postponed. One of several strategies that these lawyers use is to repeatedly obtain postponements until the witness (usually a police officer) fails to show up to testify, and then the lawyer asks for a dismissal. In many jurisdictions, the defendant has a right to one postponement without a reason. Some traffic court lawyers develop such good rapport with court personnel and the judge, however, that they can obtain a string of postponements, and the prosecution's witness is then burdened with appearing at a number of hearings. The first time the witness is absent, the lawyer requests a dismissal. Most police officers faithfully attend each time, but sooner or later another duty will conflict with the hearing date, and they will fail to appear. They know the case will be dismissed, but in reality, most officers don't care all that much about hammering minor offenders, unless at the time of the arrest you did or said something to draw attention to yourself. Many police officers and traffic court judges consider the lawyer's fee to be part of the punishment, so the dismissal of a minor offense is of little concern to them.

Another option open to you is to represent yourself at the proceeding. If you are a first-time offender; no alcohol, drugs, or injuries are involved; and your driver's license is not threatened in any way, self-representation may not be too risky. You will appear before the judge, the prosecution will present its version of the facts, you will have an opportunity to state your position, and you will probably be found guilty. Sometimes, though, the judge will reduce the fine, in many instances substantially, just because you showed interest in your case. But if you need to beat a conviction in order to maintain your current level of insurance premiums or as part of a strategy to avoid other legal consequences, representing yourself is a terrible idea. Under such circumstances, you need a lawyer. Whether or not you hire a lawyer, your options in traffic court are the following:

- Pay the fine. This involves a conviction.
- Plead guilty at arraignment.[14] The penalty is imposed at that time.
- Plead not guilty at arraignment. A trial date is set. You may be required to post bail in the amount of the potential fine.
- Plead guilty at trial. The penalty is imposed at that time.
- Plead *nolo contendere*. This is a plea of no contest to the charges. The conviction cannot be used later in a civil lawsuit to show an admission of guilt. A plea of *nolo contendere* is the same as a guilty plea, however, for purposes of your driving record.
- Plead not guilty and contest the allegations at trial.

---

14. Arraignment takes place the first time you go before the judge. At that time, the charges are read to you, and you are asked to respond with a plea of guilty or not guilty.

CHAPTER 2

THE ATTORNEY-CLIENT AGREEMENT

No matter how competent and trustworthy your lawyer may be, no matter what good and honorable reputation in the community your lawyer may have, and no matter how certain you are that you've found the right lawyer, you need a written contract to set your case properly into motion. Unfortunately, clients often discover too late that they should have clarified the attorney-client relationship and wish they had taken the time to establish the rules of the game beforehand. Even though consumer laws are supposed to protect you, it's risky to start your case without understanding who is to do what for whom and for how much money. Reading this chapter will help you negotiate and execute an attorney-client agreement with your lawyer.

1. Get It in Writing

1.1 Written versus oral agreements

The terms "fee agreement," "employment agreement," and "engagement letter" all refer to writings that establish an attorney-client relationship. In most jurisdictions, with the exception of cases that are done on a contingency-fee basis, there is no requirement that a written contract be executed between a lawyer and a client, and many lawyers do not use one.[1] Even so, a written fee agreement is a good idea for both parties, and if your lawyer does not present one, you should request that one be drafted and signed. Poorly defined notions about lawyers' services, the calculation of fees and expenses, and other matters that should be agreed on beforehand are sources of many problems that arise between lawyers and their clients. A properly drafted fee agreement defines the services to be rendered, sets out a clear structure for calculating fees, and addresses other matters that can help you and your lawyer avoid misunderstandings.

If a lawyer refuses to draft and sign a written agreement with you, look for another lawyer. If you have no written agreement, it will be your word against your lawyer's should a dispute arise. You should execute a detailed contract that describes the work to be performed, specifies the fee to be charged and the method of its calculation, indicates the expenses to be paid and by whom, and outlines the various ways that the agreement may be terminated.

1.2   Engagement letter versus contract

Even if you don't know anything about contracts, you should be able to read and understand your lawyer's proposed agreement. You simply need to focus on a few particulars. Your lawyer will present you with either a full-length fee agreement or an engagement letter with a place for you to sign at the bottom to indicate that you concur with its terms. An engagement letter can establish a valid attorney-client relationship, but such letters are often short on detail, and you should not sign one unless it comprehensively and clearly covers all important issues. If an engagement letter sets forth the major provisions that would be included in a written attorney-client agreement, it becomes an acceptable way of defining the rights and obligations of both parties. A one-paragraph letter stating that the lawyer will take your case and that you agree to pay a stated amount of money is not sufficient.

1. Some states require a written contract in all matters that create an attorney-client relationship. Others require one in specific situations. The majority, as stated in the text above, requires a written agreement only for contingency-fee cases.

The same principles apply should your lawyer present a formal contract to you. The contract should be clear and straightforward; in other words, you should be able to read and understand it without much trouble. If you don't understand a provision, ask the lawyer to explain it to you. If, after hearing the explanation, you think it's reasonable, ask that it be included in the document in the same terms that you heard in the oral version. A verbal restatement of the meaning of the provision is not sufficient; you should ensure that a clear rendition makes it into the final written agreement.

2. Important Clauses

2.1 Leaving an escape route

Anytime you enter into an agreement, you should provide a way out for yourself in the event that the relationship breaks down. You should insist upon a paragraph that defines the conditions for dismissing your lawyer, for your lawyer's withdrawal from the case, and the notification requirements for each of you should such dismissal or withdrawal take place. Changing lawyers is riddled with complicating factors for both you and your lawyer. The following issues may come into play:

- As you make the transition from your previous lawyer to a new one, it may be difficult to maintain the smooth forward progress of your case.

- Ethical requirements imposed upon your lawyer may not permit withdrawal if it would damage or endanger your case in any substantial way.

- The judge must sign an order allowing your lawyer to withdraw. Judges are sometimes reluctant to do so. They do not like to delay cases because of changes of lawyers, and often they require that the client sign the Motion to Withdraw[2] along with the lawyer. (Some lawyers require that their clients sign an undated Motion to Withdraw at the time the fee agreement is executed. They do so to prevent

---

2. A motion is a written or oral request seeking a specific ruling from the court. Such requests are made for a multitude of reasons throughout the various stages of pretrial and trial. Here the request is to withdraw from representation of the client.

hassles with clients and judges should a disagreement with the client arise.)

- When a lawyer has accumulated substantial expenses in depositions, expert-witness fees, and the like, you may not be able simply to say good-bye and go to another lawyer. You may be stuck paying the bill for those expenses long before your case ends. You might try to include a clause in the agreement stating that should you dismiss your lawyer, expenses would not be paid until the end of the case, no matter what lawyer takes the case to completion. You can imagine, though, the difficulty of insisting upon the inclusion in the fee agreement of such a provision. A lawyer may be understandably reluctant to take a case when the client is already concerned about expenses and thinking about the possibility of running off to another lawyer in the middle of the proceeding.

2.2   *Hourly fees*

When using the hourly method of billing, the lawyer charges a predetermined amount for each hour dedicated to the client's legal problem. Such rates range from $75 to $300 or more per hour. At the inception of the case, the lawyer may request a deposit of anywhere from $500 to $25,000 or more, depending upon the type and complexity of the matter to be handled. The deposit is placed in the law firm's trust account, and the fees are offset against it until it is exhausted. At that time, the lawyer will either request another deposit or bill the client on a monthly basis thereafter.

Hourly attorneys' fees are precarious for the client for a variety of reasons, especially in litigation matters. First, the lawyer gets paid whether or not the work produces positive results. The longer the case continues, the more money the lawyer makes. Even during periods of inactivity, lawyers charge for sporadic telephone calls and written status reports to apprise their clients of the progress of their cases. This built-in incentive to allow cases to drag on is one of the most objectionable aspects of hourly billing. The thoroughness of lawyers who work for hourly fees is remarkable; some of them seem to take forever to settle routine matters. Of course, those lawyers never explain to their clients why the work takes so long. If asked that question, each would have a ready answer to explain and rationalize the time spent. A natural tendency to extend the life of a case is built into the hourly fee method. Diligent clients supervise their lawyers and attempt to curb that tendency.

Second, some lawyers bill for time that was not spent working. In their view, finding faster ways to do things is increased efficiency for which they should be paid, whether or not they actually work the hours they bill. These lawyers create streamlined ways to perform a task, then bill the client as if they had done it the longer, more difficult way. Such lawyers think that since they have learned to work more efficiently, they should profit from their craftiness rather than pass the savings from their improved work methods on to their clients.

This, in my opinion, is dishonest. The lawyer may legitimately enjoy the benefits of improved work methods when the fee arrangement is fixed or contingent on a recovery, but when lawyer and client have agreed to hourly billing, the lawyer should bill only the actual hours worked on the case. The lawyer's profit, whether derived from time worked or time saved, is already built into the hourly billing rate.

Third, hourly billing lends itself to padding the bill. Padding is the arbitrary addition of time to the bill — time that was not spent working. The client cannot be physically present at every stage to observe the lawyer working on the case, so when the lawyer works for 45 minutes and records a full hour or more for that task, the client is mostly unable to discover the discrepancy.

Lawyers pad their bills for a number of reasons. Some of it is simply cheating the client. But more frequently, lawyers become infected with billing mentalities. The pressure to bill lots of hours is intense and provides great incentive to pad the bills. For example, the temptation to overcharge is strong if a lawyer wants to leave the office early to attend a grade-school softball game but does not want to work Saturday to make up the lost time. The client, unfortunately, pays the price. Padding is covered in detail in Chapter 4.

Fourth, hourly-fee rates, although arguably set by supply and demand, seem to be out of touch with reality. Few clients can afford to pay $250 per month for a lawyer's time, much less $250 per hour. Just because a lawyer's hourly rate is high, however, does not mean you should cross that name off of your list of candidates. High-priced lawyers charge not only for their superior skill levels, but also for their reputations for achieving successful outcomes and sometimes for their political connections. Some lawyers accomplish more in one telephone call than others will in months of struggling with the same problem. My experiences have shown me that the hourly rate does not matter that much in the end. The higher-priced lawyers tend to get to the heart of the problem a lot faster than the lower-priced ones, so the bottom-line fee that the client pays is frequently about the same.

You may be unable to avoid an hourly-fee arrangement with the lawyer you choose. You can, however, protect yourself from abuse by doing the following:

a) Negotiate a solid fee agreement. It's hard to complain of your lawyer's billing practices if you have not clearly defined the billing procedures to be employed in your case. The fee agreement should set forth the specific hourly rates of all lawyers, paralegal assistants, investigators, and others who are expected to work on your case. If possible, it should also specify that the work be billed in tenth-hours. A 30-second telephone call should not be billed for a quarter hour, the minimum billing unit for some lawyers.[3] Even employing a billing method whereby the lawyer's time is measured in tenth-hours, a 30-second phone call counts as six minutes. Billing in units of tenth-hours helps reduce padding and makes it easier for you to evaluate the work that has been done when you review your monthly statements.

b) Carefully review your lawyer's billing statements each month. If you have a question about the bill, ask it. Fear of confrontation or embarrassment will cost you money,

---

3. In some states, the courts have taken a stand on minimum billing times. In those jurisdictions, lawyers who bill a quarter hour must do 15 minutes of work or risk disciplinary action.

and the resentment that builds up inside you will undermine your case.

c) Insist that your lawyer include as much detail as possible in the monthly statements. The statement should contain the date each activity was performed, the name or initials of the lawyer or paralegal assistant who performed the work, a description of the activity, and the time spent on the activity.[4] The entries set out in Sample 1 contain the minimum information you need to understand the work for which your lawyer bills:

SAMPLE 1

STATEMENT

Statement, October 200_
October 3, 200_, SAA, Attended deposition of Alice Carter . . 3.5 hours
October 9, 200_, SAA, Attended depositions of George Carter and Steven Stall . . . . 4.2 hours
October 17, 200_, GAC, Research regarding Motion for Summary Judgment . . . . 3.6 hours
October 26, 200_, DCG, Drafted Motion for Summary Judgment . . . . .8 hours
October 26, 200_, DCG, Brief in Support of Motion for Summary Judgment . . . . 2.5 hours
Partner total (7.7 hours x $175.00/hour) $1,347.50
Associate total (3.3 hours x $125.00/hour) $412.50
Paralegal total (3.6 hours x $60.00/hour) . . . . $ 216.00
Total Due $1,976.00
SAA = Sara Ann Anderson, partner, fee rate $175.00 per hour
DCG = Daryl C. Grey, associate attorney, fee rate $125.00 per hour
GAC = Glenda A. Carvel, paralegal assistant, fee rate $60.00 per hour

4. Lawyers should not bill separately for secretarial time. In some states, the courts have declared secretarial time to be included in overhead, and lawyers who try to bill for it risk being disciplined.

Recording this modest amount of information should not be burdensome for your lawyer, and yet the detail is sufficient to let you know what is happening in your case and alert you to any billing abuse that might be occurring. You may request that the statements reflect even more detail than the sample suggests. Each situation is unique, but in the vast majority of cases, detailed billing is both appropriate and desirable.

It is unlikely that you will have to correct your lawyer more than once on fee matters. Most lawyers are not dishonest. They are under tremendous pressure to cover overhead costs and meet law-firm billing requirements, and when clients do not complain, the fees may become inflated. You should make it clear that you are not a Fortune 500 company and that you expect competent legal work for a reasonable fee. Lawyers want good relationships with their clients, and they will usually be fair if you voice your concerns to them and give them a chance to respond.

2.3   Contingency fees

Personal injury lawyers often charge their clients by taking a percentage of the winnings. Under such a scheme, the lawyer's fee is contingent upon the amount won at trial or agreed to in settlement and is commonly referred to as a "contingency fee."

If you can convince your lawyer to take your case on a contingent basis (i.e., in some manner link the fee to the results of the case), you will usually benefit from doing so. A contingency-fee arrangement limits your risk as a plaintiff[5] and gives your lawyer a personal stake in the action. You pay attorney's fees only if your lawyer recovers money on your behalf. A lawyer who misjudges the chances of winning a case shares in the result of that poor judgment. In the event of victory, however, most plaintiffs do not mind their lawyers' taking fat fees as long as they end up with healthy sums for themselves.

Many states require that lawyers recover expenses from their clients. Even so, plaintiffs' lawyers often pay expenses out of their own pockets as they are incurred and are repaid at the end of the

---

5. The plaintiff is the party who has filed the lawsuit and is on the offensive pursuing some remedy or satisfaction from the defendant.

case out of any settlement or recovery. The rub comes when there is no settlement or recovery from which to extract the expenses. In such instances, many lawyers prefer to forgive the debt if the rules allow them to do so. Most plaintiffs are hard pressed to pay expenses from their own funds.

Generally, the rules permit lawyers to spend money on clients for reasonable and necessary expenses of litigation, but they cannot loan money to clients or give them gifts as long as an attorney-client relationship is in effect. In the past, plaintiffs' lawyers would sometimes lend money to clients for living expenses while their cases were pending. Lawyers considered such loans necessary to keep their clients clear of financial hardship that might force premature settlements. They essentially paid their clients to keep their cases alive. The practice of loaning money was a powerful promotional tool for lawyers to attract new clients. It is now strictly prohibited in every state.

Customary contingency fees range from 25 percent to 40 percent of the net proceeds from a verdict or settlement, depending on the jurisdiction and some other factors. You may find isolated instances of contingency fees as low as 10 percent and as high as 50 percent. A common standard for personal injury cases is 33$\frac{1}{3}$ percent. For collection cases, 50 percent is not out of line, principally because the risk is great that the lawyer will earn no fee at all.

Some lawyers prefer contingency fees that vary depending on when the case is concluded. The fee set in the attorney-client agreement may be relatively low in the event of rapid settlement, higher if the case goes to trial, and higher still if an appeal is forthcoming. These schemes are fine, but many lawyers do not make clear in their agreements exactly when the next higher fee becomes applicable. For example, if a case settles after the jury selection but before the opening statements,[6] has there been a trial? At that point, the lawyer has done all of the preparation but has not completed the trial itself. The few days actually spent in the courtroom are often only the tip of the iceberg with respect to the time expended on the case, so the lawyer may try to bill at

---

6. Opening statements are presentations made by the lawyers at the beginning of a trial in which they preview the evidence that they anticipate will be presented.

the next higher fee level, as if the trial had been completed. If you decide to enter into a graduated contingency fee arrangement, the contract terms should show exactly when each fee level becomes applicable. One approach might look something like this:

1) Twenty percent of the net proceeds if the case settles before filing the lawsuit.

2) Twenty-five percent of the net proceeds if the case settles anytime after filing the lawsuit and up to 5:00 p.m. on the seventh calendar day before the case is called to trial for the first time. During this time your lawyer will take depositions, send out interrogatories,[7] file motions, attend hearings, and generally prepare your case for trial.

3) Thirty-three and one-third percent of the net proceeds if the case settles at or after 5:00 p.m. on the seventh calendar day before the case is called to trial for the first time. The judge may call several cases to trial in a given week. Not all of those cases will be tried that week, however, and your lawyer may announce to the court that you are ready for trial a number of times over a period of several months before your case is actually tried. All depositions and written discovery[8] requests must be completed before making the first announcement of ready, so the new fee level would become applicable at that time.[9]

4) Forty percent of the net proceeds if the case settles after either side has filed an appeal.

The scheme set out above is not for you to copy into your fee agreement with your lawyer. The structures of such arrangements vary from case to case. This example is simply intended to give you some ideas for negotiating a graduated contingency-fee agreement with your lawyer. You may choose to adopt a plan that is far simpler. Also, you may find the lawyer to be unreceptive to

---

7. Interrogatories are written questions submitted by one party to another for the purpose of gathering information.

8. Discovery is a formal process for investigating the facts surrounding a case. The primary discovery devices are interrogatories, depositions, requests for admission, and requests for production.

9. Some lawyers have ways of finding out in advance that a case will not go to trial that week. They may, then, make a perfunctory announcement of ready when, in fact, they are not ready for trial. If that is the case, then the next higher fee would apply, and should the case settle shortly thereafter, the lawyer might receive a windfall.

restructuring the fee arrangement, so if you want that lawyer to take your case, you may have to accept the fee structure as proposed.

Also, a contingency arrangement is not always open to contract. In some jurisdictions, statutes limit the percentages for certain types of cases or require approval of the structure of the agreement. All jurisdictions prohibit the use of contingency contracts in criminal matters and divorce proceedings.

Some self-help sources make suggestions that are imprudent with respect to negotiating contingency-fee arrangements. One of them proposes that the plaintiff (after discussing the case with a lawyer but before hiring one or filing a lawsuit) talk to the opposing party to solicit an offer and compare that offer with the prospective lawyer's estimated recovery, less attorneys' fees and expenses. This is a remarkably bad idea. Talking to anyone except your lawyer about your case is foolish. Only rarely will a defendant voluntarily make an offer that nets an amount equal to one made under the pressure of a lawsuit, and if your discussion does not bear fruit, anything you say may become testimony against you later. At trial, you may find yourself listening to words that you indeed uttered but that are stated out of context or are slightly misquoted such that their meaning is altered dramatically.

2.4 Fixed fees

A fixed fee is a set dollar amount for which the lawyer agrees to do the entire case. The client agrees to pay the fee regardless of the amount of work the lawyer performs or the outcome of the case. Criminal defense lawyers commonly set fixed fees and usually insist upon receiving all the money before they begin to work on a case. If the offense is a misdemeanor, the lawyer charges one amount; for a felony, the fee is higher. For most criminal-defense lawyers, the standard fee schedule is only a starting point. If the case has no twists that will take extra time, they charge their standard fee. But if the case is a high-publicity one with lots of extra dimensions, or a drug case in which the pockets are deep, you can bet that the lawyer will increase the fee to whatever level the market will bear.

For civil cases,[10] lawyers who have high-volume legal practices often charge fixed fees. Traffic offenses, uncontested divorces, immigration matters, formations of corporations, and simple bankruptcies are examples of concerns that are frequently handled for fixed fees. For a set fee, the lawyer does the work no matter how many hours it takes, no matter how many hearings are held, and no matter how difficult and precarious the case becomes.

Most of the risk in entering into a fixed-fee arrangement rests with the lawyer. If the case gets out of hand, the lawyer absorbs the loss. As you might imagine, lawyers are extremely cautious when setting fixed fees. Even so, the most seasoned lawyers get burned on fixed-fee cases from time to time.

The advantage to agreeing to pay a fixed fee is that you know the total legal fee before you start. One problem, though, is that if a case takes more time than anticipated, the lawyer may not continue working hard to obtain a good result. If, for instance, your uncontested divorce turns in midstream into a contested one (not at all a rare occurrence), the quality of the legal work may suddenly become more important to you, especially if substantial assets or the custody of children is involved. Therefore, if you decide to hire a lawyer on a fixed-fee basis, do so with the understanding that if the basic parameters of the case change, you may want to alter the fee arrangement. Most lawyers who do fixed-fee divorces stipulate in the attorney-client agreement that if the divorce becomes contested, the fixed fee will no longer be applicable, and an hourly fee will become operable.

2.5   Combination hourly and fixed fees

Each method of setting fees has its advantages and its drawbacks, and sometimes one can gain by employing them in combination. As mentioned in the previous section, it may be necessary to switch from a fixed fee to an hourly one in the event that the case becomes more complicated than expected. On the other hand, it may be comforting to set a limit on the hourly fees that can be charged for a given case. At the initial interview with your lawyer,

---

10. Cases that are not criminal are referred to as civil. They are often quite uncivilized, but as a matter of legal categorization, they are called civil rather than criminal.

ask for an estimate of how long the case should take and how much it should cost. Most lawyers are reluctant to do this, but if you press the issue a little, you probably can extract an approximate figure. Once you have an idea of the total, you may want to try to set an upper limit on the hourly fees, a cap that guarantees that the fees will not exceed a stated amount.

Once, an aunt of mine asked me to help her negotiate with a lawyer to draft a living trust and the other documents that accompany it. She resides in a rural community, and I thought the lawyer's hourly fee was quite reasonable at $85 per hour. I asked him to estimate the total fees for completing the work, and he responded that $850 would probably cover everything. I requested that he cap the fee at $1,000, and he agreed to do so. Later, some minor but unexpected twists came up, and the lawyer told me that he put approximately $1,600 of time into the case, $750 more than his projection. The fee, in the absence of the $1,000 cap, would have been nearly double the lawyer's estimate at the initial consultation.

2.6 Result fees

Result fees are additional fees paid to a lawyer for obtaining an exceptional outcome. Such fee arrangements are relatively rare, but they are useful in exceptional circumstances, and occur mostly in business-related matters. They are sometimes agreed to beforehand in the attorney-client agreement. At other times, they are imposed after the fact by the lawyer when it becomes apparent that the result obtained is out of proportion to the fee that would be charged on a strict hourly basis.

An example of this would be when a client needs more than the best professional efforts of a lawyer to achieve something, and the lawyer has special political connections that can be used as a springboard for obtaining those results. If the task will not require many hours of work, even a billing rate of $400 or $500 per hour might not entice the lawyer to cash in hard-earned political goodwill. If, however, the client agrees to pay an hourly fee to make the attempt, sweetened with a promise of a juicy result fee if the effort is successful, then the lawyer may enthusiastically use those brownie points on the client's behalf. Result fees are not inherently illegal, but if you use your imagination, you can easily see the wide room for abuse that such fees allow.

2.7 Retainer fees

Retainer fees are not nearly so popular as they once were. The classic view of the retainer-fee relationship is that of the faithful lawyer who has become like a member of the client's family, has represented the client for longer than anyone can remember, and has received a fixed monthly sum throughout, without respect to the amount of work done. Such relationships are riddled with problems for both sides. From the lawyer's perspective, if the client creates busywork that takes more time than the retainer fee justifies, the arrangement becomes unsatisfactory. From the client's point of view, if the lawyer does nothing during the month, the retainer seems to have been wasted.

In recent years, these fee relationships have become sophisticated to the point of nearly voiding the entire notion of the retainer fee. Just know that such agreements can be complicated, and that unless you need a lot of legal work done on an ongoing basis, retainer-fee arrangements are not for you.

2.8 Expenses

In your fee agreement, you should specify how your money is to be spent and at what point the lawyer must call you for authorization to incur additional expenses. The expenses that accompany legal work are largely unavoidable. It makes sense, though, to carefully review the expense reports and to ask as many questions as necessary to assure yourself that your money is being used wisely.

Your fee agreement should contain a clause stating that expenses will be reported to you periodically (monthly is usually preferable) in writing. It should also require that the report be rendered in sufficient detail for you to determine exactly how the money has been spent. You should ask for detailed reports on transportation, lodging, and meal expenses for your lawyer's out-of-town travel on your behalf. If your lawyer seems to be bothered by such requests, you should push for more detailed information. Chances are good that you'll find some irregularity.

3. Making the Fee Agreement a Priority

No single factor is so important to starting your case off right as negotiating a solid fee agreement. Your lawyer is in business to make money, so if you want effective representation, you must pay for that service. At the same time, you do not want to overpay for either fees or expenses, so you should execute an agreement that clearly outlines your expectations and those of your lawyer. If you properly negotiate the agreement with your lawyer, you will have done a lot toward bringing your case to a satisfactory conclusion.

PART II

CONTROLLING YOUR LAWYER

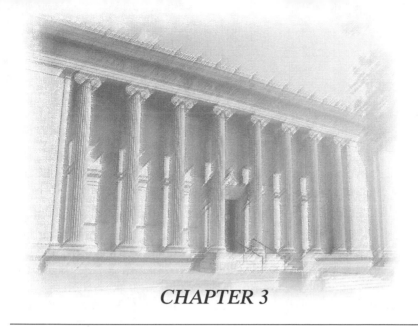

CHAPTER 3

MANAGING YOUR LAWYER

Managing a lawyer is not much different from managing an employee. Good managers do not allow even the most responsible, trustworthy, and mature individuals to work for long periods without supervision. They may pay extra attention to employees whose performances are marginal, but they monitor the activities of good employees as well. Like a good employee, a lawyer needs a nudge or a pat on the back from time to time. If you play your role as manager correctly, you will maximize your lawyer's productivity, minimize the complications in your case, and vastly enhance your chances of success. Success is achieving the best possible outcome given the facts of the case and the applicable law.

You should not assume your lawyer to be self-motivated, thus requiring no supervision. Most lawyers are self-starters, but not all of them are. Even if your lawyer appears to be working diligently, though, you should maintain a high profile in all of the activities that take place. Your lawyer needs your help to do a good job for you. The more you know about your case, the better your lawyer will be able to use you as a tool and resource.

In order to be effective at managing your lawyer, you must —

1) ensure that the monetary incentive is adequate to motivate your lawyer to work, and

2) communicate openly and honestly with your lawyer as your case proceeds toward its conclusion.

Some lawyers are not induced to work harder by the prospect of making more money, but most of them are. When adequate monetary incentives are absent, many lawyers will not render the best service possible. If, however, the incentives are solidly in place from the beginning, your case will likely take a high position on your lawyer's list of things to do. In many instances, creative schemes that protect your interests and motivate your lawyer to do a good job can be woven into the agreement.

Theoretically, contingency arrangements accomplish this result. When hourly fees apply, you might insert a bonus for a favorable result or negotiate a reduced fee for an unfavorable one. The fee should be reasonable and fair, but not necessarily low. Stable business arrangements give good value to both sides.

The second component of effective lawyer management, communicating with your lawyer, is just as important as the first. Maintaining open communication regarding every phase of your case is a key to achieving a favorable outcome. Make clear at the outset that you intend to make informed decisions based on your lawyer's recommendations and on common sense. Most lawyers enjoy working for clients who want to understand their own cases, and usually they will be accommodating. Of course, some of the legal procedures may appear complicated, and you may have to accept your lawyer's recommendations regarding such matters on blind faith. Even when obscure concepts muddy the water a little, however, your lawyer should be able to explain them in terms that you understand. Most of the rules make sense without necessarily comprehending all of their subtleties and implications.

A lawyer works for a client much like a construction contractor works for a homeowner. If you hire a contractor to remodel your house, the contractor first listens to your explanation of what you want. You, in turn, listen to the contractor's explanation of your options and what each one will cost. You carefully consider all recommendations and supporting arguments and ask thoughtful questions before making your final decision. In like fashion, when you begin to work with your lawyer, you first disclose all the facts — the incidents or events that brought you to the lawyer's office in the first place. Your lawyer explains your options to you and makes a recommendation, you ask questions about each option, and you select the one that best suits you. If you and your lawyer work together and communicate openly, you will achieve the best possible result in your case.

1. Common Errors

Clients frequently commit one or more of the following errors:

- They telephone their lawyers too often.
- They dwell on the negative aspects of their cases.
- They expect their lawyers to achieve unrealistic goals.
- They try to make friends with their lawyers.
- They excessively manage their lawyers' activities.

Telephoning too often costs you money and your lawyer's respect. Some clients call their lawyers several times a day, even during periods when their cases are inactive. Such persistence is counterproductive. After a few pointless conversations, the lawyer may become gun-shy and begin to avoid taking the client's calls. Telephoning more often than necessary also runs up legal fees. If you work diligently to understand what is supposed to happen next in your case, you will know when and how often to call.

Dwelling on the negative aspects of your case — a hearing that did not go well, mounting expenses, repeated delays — serves to undermine your relationship with your lawyer. Lawyers, like other human beings, become ineffective when they are repeatedly criticized for the same mistakes. Few cases proceed without glitches, and your lawyer's judgment may at times seem wanting. If you identify an error, you should let your lawyer know that you are aware of it to ensure that the same thing doesn't happen again. As quickly as possible, though, you should put the incident behind you and focus on the future of your case. Browbeating your lawyer over a poor decision normally will not improve your chances of success. Of course, you should document serious errors with letters to your lawyer so that you have a record of every anomaly. If such errors compound, you may even have to change lawyers and later file a lawsuit for malpractice. If it's a minor mistake, however, forget about it and get on with your case.

Asking your lawyer to achieve unrealistic goals can make you appear foolhardy. No lawyer wants a client who constantly dreams of huge jury awards far out of proportion to the real merit of the case. Some clients expect their lawyers to convert minor injuries magically into million-dollar settlements. Keeping your desires in check will allow you to work far more effectively with your lawyer and will make the result more palatable when you receive it.

You should avoid making friends with your lawyer, at least until your case is over. A congenial relationship is important, but you should not be so amicable that complacency sets in. Try to maintain some psychological distance so that you can be critical and demanding when necessary. If you discover that you have a lot in common with your lawyer, and you think that a genuine friendship might develop, you can investigate that possibility after your case is over.

Worried clients sometimes attempt to micromanage their lawyers' activities, which undermines the work and inflates the fees. Constantly hounding your lawyer is a nuisance; responsible lawyers do not like to charge for unnecessary client contact, but they will if you insist upon initiating it. In addition, pressure from clients can cause lawyers to do things that are against their better judgment. That's why it's so important that you learn about your case. Only if you understand what is going on will you know when to push your lawyer and when to go easy.

The key to avoiding these errors is to have an organized approach to supervising your lawyer. Maintaining a balanced attitude toward your case is the best way to develop a stable attorney-client relationship. This is far more difficult to do than to discuss. The remainder of this chapter provides some concrete ideas regarding how you can attain and maintain such an attitude.

2. Taking Charge

Below are some specific suggestions that will help you stay abreast of your case and win the respect of your lawyer. The ideas are equally applicable to litigation[1] and non-litigation matters, although their non-litigation applications may be so simple as to make some of them unnecessary. The litigation process is intimidating and confusing to most people, so the emphasis here is on working with your lawyer before and during trial.

2.1 Construct a calendar of events

At the outset of your case, you and your lawyer should construct a calendar of anticipated events with an approximate date corresponding to each one. Once you understand how the overall case is likely to unfold, you will be better prepared to make informed decisions as your case moves along. You should leave your first planning conference with at least a rough draft of such a calendar.

The first time you attempt to make a calendar, you may not be able to predict some of the events accurately. You may be fairly certain, for example, that the opposing party will request that you produce documents, but you will probably not know when that step will happen. Put it on your calendar anyway. You can change the date or eliminate the entire entry as the case begins to take shape. Your calendar is a tool for you to use throughout the litigation process. You should constantly update it as your case progresses. Some of the events you put on it may not take place at all. Others may happen at times far different from your lawyer's projection. New ones may appear that you will have to add. If you continually revise and update your calendar, it will contribute substantially to your understanding of your case.

Sample 2 is an example of a calendar for a civil case in state court and should help orient you regarding the format and construction of your own calendar of events.

---

1. Litigation is the process of carrying on a lawsuit.

SAMPLE 2
CALENDAR OF EVENTS

EVENT	APPROXIMATE DATE
Plaintiff sends demand letter	May 200_
Plaintiff files lawsuit	July 200_
Defendant files answer*	August 200_
Conference between the parties**	September 200_
Plaintiff sends interrogatories	October 200_
Plaintiff sends requests for production of documents	October 200_
Defendant sends interrogatories	November 200_
Defendant sends requests for production of documents	November 200_
Defendant deposes plaintiff	January 200_
Plaintiff deposes defendant	January 200_
Defendant answers interrogatories†	February 200_
Defendant produces documents	February 200_
Plaintiff answers interrogatories	March 200_
Plaintiff produces documents	March 200_
Defendant deposes plaintiff's expert witness	June 200_
Plaintiff deposes defendant's expert witness	August 200_

* The answer is a document filed by the defendant that responds to the plaintiff's charges, usually by denying them, and sets forth the defendant's defenses and counterclaims.

** In some states, the parties must meet informally before any discovery is done to exchange information and make a discovery plan. The plan is then submitted to the judge for approval.

† Delays are common with respect to answering interrogatories and requests for production of documents. Although the rules require responses within a few weeks in most jurisdictions, the two months I have allowed here for those responses reflect an optimism that would make some lawyers chuckle.

SAMPLE 2 — Continued

Plaintiff sends requests for admissions††	September 200_
Defendant answers admissions	October 200_
Settlement conference	December 200_
Final interview and preparation of witnesses	February 200_
Pretrial hearing	March 200_
Trial	March 200_

†† Each party may request that the opposition admit certain facts. The party receiving the requests must admit, deny, or object to the assertion in each one. Admissions eliminate facts from controversy and narrow the disputed issues in the case.

Sample 2 is just an example. Events in litigation are unique to each case, and yours may require many more events and much more time. Lawyers who have reviewed this calendar have commented that the time frames are optimistic for civil litigation in most jurisdictions. At every stage you should expect delays. Depositions and hearings may be repeatedly rescheduled to accommodate all of the participants involved. Responses to interrogatories and documentary requests may come after one or more extensions of deadlines. And depending upon the level of congestion of the court's docket, a trial date may be impossible to obtain in less than a couple of years from the time that it is requested.

As you construct your calendar, insist that your lawyer be as realistic as possible in estimating the dates of the various events. The more realistic you are about each date, the more useful the calendar will be for administering your case. You will use it for tracking your lawyer's efforts throughout the pretrial phase. Remember, though, no matter how well you construct your calendar and attempt to foresee all of the possible events and the likely delays for each of them, each stage of the case may take longer than you anticipate. Surprises always seem to crop up along the way. It is amazing how a month, another month, and yet another can slip by with little or no activity on your case. Just stay calm, periodically update your calendar of events with your lawyer, and firmly push forward toward the trial.

2.2   Telephone your lawyer periodically for updates on your case

Sometimes your case may be inactive for several months at a time. Using your calendar of events, you should be able to identify these inactive intervals as they approach. You needn't maintain much contact with your lawyer during these slow times; checking in once every month or two may be sufficient. When your case is active, however, it may be necessary to telephone your lawyer as often as every day. Common sense must be your guide.

You should end each telephone conversation with your lawyer by asking when you should call again and what will happen in the meantime. Then keep your side of the bargain and call your lawyer on the agreed date. Each time you call, you can begin the conversation with a reminder that at the end of the last telephone conference you agreed to talk on that day. Next, ask about the status of the case. If you establish a pattern of responsible behavior, your lawyer will understand that you take such agreements seriously and expect timely action on promises made to you.

2.3   Confirm your decisions in writing

After every important conference with your lawyer, briefly outline in a letter your understanding of the options presented to you, and indicate the one that you have selected. Include clear instructions to go forward with the selected option even if you have already given oral instructions to do so. This practice documents your decisions in the case and gives your lawyer an opportunity to correct you if your respective understandings do not mesh. You can refer to the letter later in the event that your lawyer does not follow your instructions. Written instructions will motivate your lawyer more than verbal ones. Your lawyer will know you are making a paper trail that serves to ensure things are done in accordance with your wishes and that sets the stage for a malpractice action should one become necessary.

2.4   Visit your lawyer's office

Every few months during slow periods, and perhaps once a month during active periods, you should visit your lawyer's office to briefly discuss the status of your case and review the file. Depending upon the terms of your fee agreement, you may be charged for the lawyer's time, so do not linger.

Be as businesslike as possible, and get right to the point. But do not let your lawyer simply inform you of the status of the case; after you have been verbally briefed, ask for a quiet place to review the file. Don't forget to ask if the file is complete. Selected documents or sections of the file may be in other places in the office waiting for someone to work on them or insert them into a file folder. Each time you review the file, you should take notes, recording the titles of the documents that appear there and the dates that they were either filed with the court or mailed from the lawyer's office.

You should date your notes and keep them in a safe place at home. After each visit you can compare your new notes with the ones from the previous review. You will learn a great deal about your case from these file reviews. A solid understanding of each phase of your case is paramount to the effective management of your lawyer.

A disorganized file may be an indication that your lawyer is not on top of every aspect of your case. If the documents are in disarray, you may have cause to suspect that your lawyer could do a better job. Be advised, though, that not all disorganized lawyers are bad lawyers. A disorderly file, while it may be a fair indicator of sloppy work, does not necessarily mean that your lawyer has lost control of your case. Some good lawyers have offices that look as if hurricanes hit them. Reviewing your lawyer's file is one tool available to you for the control and management of your case. It is, however, only one among many, and you should view it as such. Your lawyer may detest your practice of reviewing the file. So be it! The file is an important tool in your management of your lawyer's activities. You should insist upon reading it on a regular basis. It will help you tremendously to do so.

2.5 Visit the courthouse to review the court clerk's file

Copies of all the papers that have been filed by both sides in your case are on file at the court clerk's[2] office for the county in which the lawsuit is pending. All you have to do is go to that office in the courthouse and ask to see the file. You may need the case number to find it. As you review its contents, you should take notes, recording the name of each document and the date it was filed at the court clerk's office. Be sure to label and date your notes. The information in the court clerk's file is useful for verifying what your lawyer tells you about the progress of the case, delays, and so forth. Be advised, though, that not all documents generated by your lawyer are filed at the court clerk's office. Research memoranda, briefs on legal points, general correspondence, and discovery documents will not be found there. You must review your lawyer's file, as well, in order to get a feel for the status of the whole case.

In some states, you can retrieve information about the documents that have been filed in your case from the Internet. The court clerk's office will provide you with the address to a Web site on which you will find a complete list of the documents that have been filed and the date of each filing. You will probably not be able to view the contents of the documents; for that, you'll have to go physically to the courthouse to obtain the file. The filing information is useful, though, to verify that your lawyer is telling you the truth about activity that has taken place in your case.

2.6 Attend all hearings and depositions

You should consistently demonstrate your concern about your case to the judge, your lawyer, and opposing counsel. Showing that you are not afraid to face day-to-day matters is extremely important. You can accomplish this, in part, by attending all hearings and depositions. Showing up at these events will give you a working knowledge of the facts and the law applicable to your case and will help you understand some of the hurdles that confront your lawyer. Certain hearings, though, may be held in the judge's private chambers, and you may not be allowed to attend.

2. The name of the office that records the documents and keeps the file may vary from jurisdiction to jurisdiction. Possible names include District Court Clerk, County Court Clerk, Circuit Court Clerk, and others.

The matter for discussion sometimes lends itself to an informal setting, and privacy can be appropriate. In some situations, you may want to insist that a hearing be held in open court so that you can be present. If you stay abreast of your case, you will know when such private hearings are justified.

Whether the hearing is held in open court or in the judge's chambers, you should be close by. If it is held in the judge's chambers, and you are not invited to enter, wait patiently in the hallway outside where everyone can see you. Ask your lawyer to mention to the judge that you are present. The psychological credit you receive for being there will be nearly the same as it would have been had the hearing been public. The important thing is to show your willingness to face your opponent and your determination to engage in the battle.

2.7 Use common sense

No matter what phase your case is in, common sense must be your guide. If you educate yourself with respect to the facts, law, and procedure, you will be better prepared to assist your lawyer in making decisions, but such knowledge must be tempered with common sense. Many decisions require no knowledge of the law at all. In some instances, common sense alone may be sufficient to put an important phase of the case behind you.

You should also have the savvy to accept your lawyer's common-sense suggestions. If your lawyer recommends a shortcut for the resolution of your problem, you should seriously consider taking it. Practical solutions to legal problems often save money. If the advice is good, pay the bill and go away smiling.

2.8 Study your case

If you do your homework, by the time your case goes to trial you will understand the facts that are to be presented just as well as your lawyer does. You will also have a feel for the legal obstacles that your lawyer has encountered along the way and the problems that are likely to emerge at trial. This is not to say that you should second-guess your lawyer by learning to do the work yourself.

Your job is not to be the lawyer, but rather to know enough about your case to comprehend fully the advice that you receive.

Knowledge about your case is also helpful if a settlement offer is made before trial. If you understand the problems that your lawyer is likely to encounter in court, you will be better prepared to analyze the risks involved in going forward. You will also be more competent to assign a money value to your case, and settlement negotiations will make more sense to you. Understanding the hazards involved in proceeding to trial will make you more confident about your decision to accept a settlement offer, reject it, or make a counteroffer. Possessing such knowledge is preferable to accepting on blind faith your lawyer's recommendation to settle your case or take it to trial.

For example, if you and your lawyer anticipate that the jury will dislike one of your witnesses, you must weigh the value of that testimony against the risk of offending one or more of the jurors. If your other evidence is strong, you may choose to omit the testimony because you think you can win your case without it and you prefer not to run the risk of presenting an undesirable witness. If your other evidence is weak, however, you may have no choice but to present the testimony. Your lawyer goes through this sort of analysis many times during trial, and for better or worse, makes hundreds of decisions based on the situations presented there. If you are involved in this process and understand the difficulties encountered in making such decisions, you will be able to participate in a constructive way. Most lawyers are happy to include an informed, reasonable client in the decision-making process.[3]

Make sure that you are involved in each phase of the proceeding. Doing so can mean the difference between winning and losing. Whatever the outcome, though, your close attention to each event will ensure that your case is presented in the best way possible. If you communicate with your lawyer and stay in touch with the issues, you will greatly increase your chances of success.

---

3. The American Bar Association's Model Rules of Professional Conduct make trial tactics the exclusive province of the lawyer. Although the client should be consulted, the lawyer is not obligated to follow the client's instructions in such matters.

3. Hurry up and Wait

One of the biggest headaches for clients involved in lawsuits is the waiting. Most clients, once they employ a lawyer, want to proceed to trial rapidly. Unfortunately, in many jurisdictions a case can take several years to go to trial. Your lawyer should not, however, simply file the lawsuit, sit back, and wait. Important work must be done throughout the life of the case, and if your lawyer allows too many other matters to take priority over yours, it may take three or four years to reach trial instead of one or two. Experienced lawyers know how to push a case forward. When a case is worked properly, often the only limitation for reaching trial expeditiously is the court's trial schedule.

Whenever your case is inactive, your lawyer should be able to articulate why waiting is appropriate. With the exception of purposeful delays accomplished for tactical reasons, your lawyer should rarely be just waiting. The procedural ball should always be placed in the opponent's or the judge's court, then brief idle periods may be justified.

Your approach to delays will depend, among other things, upon whether you are a plaintiff or a defendant. If you are a defendant in a civil proceeding, lengthy delays can improve your chances of winning. Defense lawyers employ all sorts of crafty devices to retard the progress of their cases for months or even years. As time passes, the defendant's chances of success improve. Witnesses move, become ill, die, forget the details of the occurrence, or become disenchanted with their involvement in the action. Physical or documentary evidence may be misplaced or destroyed. The plaintiff may even tire of waiting and lose interest in the case, or stop completely because escalating expenses seem to be consuming anticipated returns. And jurors, once they learn the dates of the occurrences upon which the lawsuit is based, sometimes take on a let-bygones-be-bygones attitude and award little or nothing to the plaintiff. The whole thing has a tendency to get stale over time.

Delays have the opposite effect on the plaintiff. Every holdup reduces the plaintiff's chances of attaining a fair result. The defendant's lawyer often adopts delay as the primary defensive strategy. A good plaintiff's lawyer always remains on the offensive, pushing the case along and obliging the defense to react. If the defense persists in the use of dilatory tactics, sanctions[4] are available for the plaintiff's lawyer to force responses.

But the notion that delay generally favors the defense has its exceptions, and one of them is when the plaintiff's case is entirely frivolous. In that situation, the passage of time may actually add credibility to the plaintiff's case. Jurors, and some judges, may believe that a case that has survived for a year or two must have some merit. Plaintiffs' lawyers know that a case takes on additional value with every legal challenge they successfully repel. Lawsuits with virtually no factual or legal basis that survive a number of pretrial motions sometimes end up settling for surprisingly large amounts of money. Lawyers who file groundless lawsuits rely upon the judges' poor decisions, biased rulings, and reluctance to impose sanctions.[5]

One way to help reduce the delay in your case is to attend all hearings and depositions, if you can. You should tell your lawyer that you want to be notified in advance of every event that takes place. Lawyers tend to be better prepared if they know their clients will be present. Also, judges sometimes extend subtle courtesies to parties who show interest in and concern for their cases. In addition, lawyers may be less likely to repeatedly reschedule events if their clients must be informed of each postponement.

You should not be shy about asking why a hearing or deposition has been postponed. At the outset, you constructed a calendar of events so that you could track the progress of your case according to an approximate timetable. If the time varies somewhat from that, don't worry. Your lawyer has no control over the court or opposing counsel. But if the delays are numerous, and the timetable seems to be lengthening considerably, insist upon a complete explanation from your lawyer.

---

4. Sanctions are the imposition of a penalty or fine by the court.

5. Judges hesitate to impose sanctions against lawyers, especially in jurisdictions in which the judiciary is elected. They are ever aware that even uncooperative lawyers, come election time, may be counted on for campaign contributions.

4. Settlement

Your lawyer should inform you of any settlement offer, no matter how absurd it appears to be, and give you a recommendation as to whether or not to accept it. The final decision to accept or reject the offer is yours. You have no obligation to follow your lawyer's recommendation, although it makes good sense to evaluate it carefully before rejecting it.

Even though you and your lawyer are joint-venture partners in the lawsuit and your lawyer's firm may have invested tens of thousands of dollars of its own funds in your case, you alone have the final word regarding settlement. If you have doubts about your lawyer's good judgment or suspect that some self-serving motive is entwined in the settlement recommendation, you can simply reject the offer. On the other hand, if you have succeeded in maintaining a harmonious working relationship with your lawyer and you are satisfied that the recommendation is based upon sound professional judgment, you will probably want to follow it.

5. Managing Your Business Lawyer

Conceiving, negotiating, drafting, revising, and executing contracts raises a great deal of controversy between business clients and lawyers. Frequently, neither lawyer nor client understands the role that the other should play in the contract-negotiation process. On one hand, business clients believe the lawyer's approach to negotiating and drafting contracts to be overly technical and generally designed to cost too much money and break good deals. Lawyers, on the other hand, think of business clients as sloppy, tending to gloss over important details that may come back to haunt them later. Both are partially correct and partially in error.

Because of their distrust of lawyers, and also because of their own healthy egos, many business clients avoid legal consultation until they are well into contract negotiations. The client, out of fear that the lawyer's over-attention to detail will interfere with the negotiation, waits until the main elements of the bargain have been established to seek counsel. The lawyer is then brought into the negotiation and is sometimes miffed at having been left out of the early stages of the negotiation process. The lawyer may privately believe the client to be an idiot for not having considered all aspects of the deal beforehand.[6]

An example of the antipathy that a client can feel for a lawyer's advice came up with one of my clients a few years ago. One day, the client sent me a fax of a proposed agreement and a handwritten note asking me to write a contract for the repair and renovation of a number of railroad cars. The client was to travel to the repair facility the next day; the cars were already en route. I called the owner of the repair facility to obtain some additional details, drafted the best contract I could with such limited time and information, and faxed it to my client's hotel. I included a letter stating that I believed the negotiated details, especially the pricing structure, to be precariously incomplete and general. I went on to say that if I were included in the negotiation, the agreement could be improved a lot. My client and I talked briefly that evening by telephone, and he confirmed that he had received my draft contract. I restated my concerns about the pricing structure, but he did not invite me to participate in the negotiation.

I did not hear from him for about two months, and I had forgotten about the matter, when I received an urgent telephone call from him requesting my assistance. He informed me that some of the railroad cars had been repaired and released, but that others were being held at the repair facility pending payment, and that he had been billed far more than he had calculated by his interpretation of the pricing structure in the agreement. He and the owner of the repair facility had exchanged harsh words over the pricing. The owner had refused to release any more cars until he received full payment. My client wanted to sue. He made no mention of the contract that I had sent him or of my letter.

When I received a copy of the agreement he had signed, I was surprised to find that he had ignored my draft contract as well as the sketchy one he had sent me initially and had signed a third version that I had never seen. The signed contract contained the

6. I am always amazed to learn of clients who present signed contracts to lawyers for review. At that point, if something was omitted from the contract or a clause was worded in an unclear or risky fashion, it's too late to do anything about it.

same problems I had cited in my letter to him, plus some additional ones. After further negotiations that cost thousands of dollars in attorneys' fees and many additional thousands in lost use of the railroad cars held hostage by the repair facility, the parties settled on a price that was not satisfactory to either of them.

My client should not have attempted to negotiate and write the contract alone. What he should have done was create a negotiation team to include a crusty old employee who was familiar with every nut and bolt that goes into a railroad car, himself, and me. The three of us should have met beforehand to nail down the exact details of the railroad-car renovation. Then he should have included us in the negotiation with the owner of the repair facility. The renovation of the cars was costly, so it would have merited some attention in advance to the details.

A contract is not drafted for the deals that go well, but rather for those that go awry. A well-drafted agreement sets forth the obligations of the parties, channels their activities, and makes them aware of how they must perform in order for each to comply with the expectations of the other. But successful performance is not the true test of a good contract; both parties might fulfill their obligations even in the absence of a written document.

What tests a contract is a challenge to its provisions in court. A nonlawyer acquaintance of mine once drafted a contract on his own and boasted to me later, "See, I told you I could do it. Everything went just fine." What he failed to realize was that he could not know whether his contract would hold up unless the provisions that he had written were actually challenged in court. He was shooting in the dark. In that instance, he was fortunate that the other party performed in good faith according to the spirit of their agreement. His contract drafting skills were not tested.

Contracts should be drafted both to guide the performances of the parties and to define their rights and obligations in the event things do not proceed as anticipated. Negotiating and drafting a contract forces the parties to consider the problems that could surface during their performances and to find solutions to them.

Before entering contract negotiations, you should discuss with your lawyer what your relative roles will be in the conception, negotiation, drafting, revision, and execution of the agreement. Identify your goals in the clearest terms possible, making sure that your lawyer knows exactly what you want to accomplish. Bring your lawyer into the negotiation early in order to warn you of potential pitfalls in the agreement. The dialogue between you and your lawyer can be extremely useful for defining the boundaries within which both of you must work to conceive and negotiate the deal. As a lawyer friend of mine has stated, "In contract negotiations, the business person is the accelerator, and the lawyer is the brake. Both are necessary to reach the destination."

After the two of you have discussed the anticipated terms of the agreement, your lawyer should draft the document in rough form. This initial draft should contain clauses favoring your position as much as possible within the bounds of the deal you would like to strike. Keep in mind that at this point your lawyer may not have spoken to anyone on the other side of the agreement and will probably not have enough information to create a final draft. Nor will your lawyer necessarily have a feel for your leverage in the negotiation. In early drafts of an agreement, this lack of information often creates imperfections that cause inexperienced clients to become disenchanted with their lawyers. What savvy clients know, however, is that using a lawyer to negotiate and draft a contract is a process. They understand that they must participate with their lawyers in that process if they expect to achieve optimum results. If they work as a team, they can present a unified front to the other party. An agreement that grows out of such cooperation will be well conceived and accurately reflected in the final written document.

As soon as the first draft is ready, you and your lawyer should meet to discuss each provision in the document. Some paragraphs of the draft agreement will be acceptable, others unnecessary, some unrealistic, and still others highly desirable but impossible to negotiate. Then you must make the business decision, based on your lawyer's advice regarding any legal consequences, to eliminate or change those paragraphs that do not mesh with your goals for the negotiation. During the negotiation, you may be forced to make additions or deletions to the agreement according to the demands of the other party. Such changes are acceptable as long as they are made thoughtfully and with full attention to detail. Your lawyer's job is to advise you of the risks of including clauses in or excluding them from the contract. Your job is to take that information and apply it to the business deal at hand.

Once you have fully discussed the first draft of the contract with your lawyer, and that draft has been revised, you are ready to discuss the provisions with the other parties. Depending on the circumstances, you may or may not wish to present your draft contract during the initial negotiation. Some clients ask their lawyers to create several draft agreements, each with different clauses, and then they present one or more of the drafts according to the direction that the negotiation takes. Others ask that various versions of the controversial clauses be drafted on separate sheets of paper, and then they present only the ones that make sense in the context of the conversation. If the other party does not object, you may include your lawyer in the discussion. Sometimes it may be appropriate to instruct your lawyer to listen and not talk. In that event, you can exchange ideas during breaks or at lunch, out of the hearing of the other party.

Any way you choose to do it, you will be well served to keep your lawyer informed as the contract negotiation proceeds. If you and your lawyer fully understand your respective roles, the result can be a well-negotiated, finely crafted contract that accurately reflects the goals of the parties and protects everyone involved.

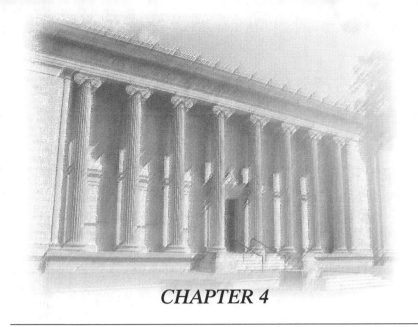

CHAPTER 4

MINIMIZING THE ABUSE

The sections that follow reveal some of the ways that lawyers abuse their clients. Many of the methods are technically legal; others, blatantly illegal. All lack moral virtue. Such activity is difficult to stop, and it will continue until consumers become aware of it and the reasons behind it.

As licensed professionals, lawyers owe a variety of duties to the public. Each state grants law licenses to lawyers in exchange for promises to perform legal work according to prescribed standards that include ethical billing practices. Some lawyers, however, consider their law licenses to be permits to charge enough to become wealthy without respect to the real value of the services rendered. Many law students candidly admit that their principal goal in becoming lawyers is to make money. Lawyers of the 21st century will make several times the earnings of the average worker.

In this chapter, I explain the methods lawyers use to overcharge their clients. It's no joke when you pay $100 to $300 an hour or more for legal services. Many people don't make that much money in an entire day, so when they spend it they want it to count. In order to protect yourself from abuse, and to get the biggest bang for your buck, you need to understand the nature of the abuse that may be directed at you.

1. Padding the Bills

Padding is the practice of adding time that is not worked to the client's bill. It has become a widespread method of overcharging clients; many lawyers routinely pad their bills in some form or another. The senior partners in the movie *The Firm*, unbeknownst to the star junior lawyer, padded the law firm's bills by adding time to each billing entry. In real life, though, few lawyers are so unsophisticated and blatantly dishonest as to pad their bills in such a crude, risky fashion.

Padding is done in at least seven different ways. One method is to establish a minimum billing time, perhaps a quarter hour, for any work done.[1] Thus, if the lawyer charges $150 per hour, a three-minute telephone call to the opposing lawyer to change the time for a deposition counts as one quarter hour and costs the client $37.50. This works out to an effective billing rate of $750 per hour! One lawyer I know begins each workday with a series of short telephone calls. Frequently, he is able to bill four or five hours or even more by 10:00 a.m. Other members of the firm admire him for leading in hours billed to the clients while still leaving the office each day in the middle of the afternoon.

The second way that legal fees are padded is by assigning a fixed amount of billing time to each task and then finding ways to perform those tasks quicker while still charging the fixed amount. A common justification for this practice is that a creative lawyer should benefit from improved efficiency. This may seem like a fair statement, but lawyers' hourly rates have steadily increased over time, so the more efficient work methods are already factored into the higher prices. If the agreement is that the lawyer will work for an hourly fee, the entire savings from improved efficiency should be passed on to the client.

---

1. Lawyers who use a quarter hour as their minimum billing time, when challenged, will nearly always lower that minimum to a tenth-hour.

A lawyer may decide, for instance, to bill a half hour for answering a lawsuit that contains no counterclaims or other complications. Drafting a simple answer probably took a half hour or even longer the first time the lawyer did one as a novice, but an experienced lawyer can dictate one from memory in a couple of minutes. Once the form for a routine answer is saved in the word processor, the lawyer dictates only the relevant variable information, and a secretary or paralegal assistant inputs it into the form. The lawyer then bills the standard half hour for drafting the document. In the same breath, the lawyer instructs the secretary or paralegal assistant to send standard interrogatories and requests for production[2] of documents to the opposition, and then bills perhaps 1.5 hours for that work. The assistant creates the documents, the lawyer signs them, and the assistant sends them out. A lawyer who understands how to use forms efficiently can bill several hours for the receipt and review of a simple lawsuit, the filing of an answer, and the drafting of discovery requests. The lawyer's total time invested in the preparation of those documents, however, may be less than 15 minutes.

Senior lawyers like this method of overcharging. They accept the cases, and after billing the routine initial activities (drafting answers, sending out interrogatories, requesting the production of documents, and notifying witnesses of depositions) for inflated amounts of time, pass them on to unwitting junior lawyers. Once the easy billing has been skimmed off the top, the senior lawyer is glad to be rid of the case; from that point forward, inflated billing becomes more difficult, so the senior lawyer prefers to move on to more fertile ground. The junior lawyer who inherits the case may struggle later to keep the total fee below the estimate quoted by the senior lawyer at the initial consultation. Frequently, the relentless draining of fees early on by the senior lawyer creates the problem. To add insult to injury, the junior lawyer is often stuck with the unpleasant task of informing the client that the fees will exceed the estimate.

Many junior lawyers never figure out that they have been duped when they receive cases with the fees stripped from them

---

2. A request for production is a written request that the opposing party turn over specified documents or other items for inspection or copying.

in this fashion. This practice not only cheats clients but also short-changes young lawyers. Junior lawyers look up to senior lawyers as mentors who set the standards for the professional and ethical attitudes of the future. The sad result of this mentorship is that when junior lawyers become senior partners, they tend to treat their own clients and junior lawyers in the same fashion.

The third way to pad the bill is simply to add some time to each activity as it is completed. Here is a normal day at the office for lawyer Wanda Jones. Wanda arrives at the office at 8:15 a.m. She spends 50 minutes in a meeting with another lawyer and charges one hour to the client. Then she attends a hearing that takes 10 minutes, with 15 additional minutes to walk to and from the courthouse, and records one hour. Upon returning to her office, she receives three five-minute telephone calls. She charges a quarter hour each for the first two calls and a half hour for the third, because the conversation seemed exceptionally productive and the case should settle soon. She receives two small lawsuits from a corporate client, reads them, and dictates instructions to her secretary to send out answers and standard interrogatories. The review and dictation take 30 minutes, and she bills two hours. Then she begins research on a motion that she's planning to file later in the week. She works on that for an hour and forty-five minutes and charges two hours. She spends an hour and a half at lunch with a friend.

After lunch, she completes the research in an additional hour and 40 minutes and records two hours. Then she attends three short administrative hearings at the building across the street. She waits 20 minutes to be heard, spends 10 minutes at each hearing, and charges one hour to each client for a total of three hours. She telephones a friend to set up a dinner engagement for Friday evening, and they chat for 20 minutes before hanging up. Finally, she leaves the office at 4:20 p.m. to take her daughter to a softball game. Leaving early is no problem, because she has billed a cool 12 hours for the day — more than enough to make the partners happy and keep her on track for a sizable bonus at the end of the year.

Wanda's clients paid for her time at lunch, at the softball game, on the telephone with her friend, and more. Wanda charged 12 hours for the day, but her actual productive time working for her clients was less than 7 hours.

The fourth method of padding the bills is double billing. Double billing means to charge two clients for the same time worked. It is accomplished in several ways. For instance, a lawyer may charge a client eight hours for a day trip to another city to attend a hearing. Then, in the airport, airplane, taxicab, and hotel, the lawyer may work on other cases and bill those clients for portions of the same eight hours. This also takes place at the courthouse. Hearings and trials involve a lot of waiting time, and many lawyers take advantage of that time by working on other matters. Cellular telephones and laptop computers have made this practice easier and more profitable than ever before. Lawyers also double bill by doing research that applies to more than one case. I know one lawyer who has billed five hours for the same research project countless times. He has made thousands of dollars over the years for those initial five hours in the library!

The fifth way that lawyers pad their bills is by billing up. Billing up happens when a senior lawyer assigns work to an associate lawyer or a paralegal assistant and charges the time as if the senior lawyer had done the work. For example, a senior lawyer whose normal billing rate is $175 per hour may assign a ten-hour research project to a paralegal assistant whose billing rate is $60 per hour. The firm should bill ten hours at $60 per hour, or $600, for the project. Instead, the lawyer bills ten hours at $175 per hour, or $1,750, and the statement reflects that the lawyer did the work. Many lawyers bill up from time to time, and it's tough to catch them at it, but you should be aware of the practice.

The sixth way lawyers pad their bills is by charging for overhead items that are already built into their hourly fees, such as secretarial time. Overhead consists of the general, continuing costs involved in running a business. Amounts paid for rent, maintenance, utilities, taxes, and secretaries' salaries are overhead and should not be billed separately from attorneys' fees. In some states, charging for overhead items is strictly prohibited and can become the subject of disciplinary action. Some lawyers also tack margins onto their bills for photocopies, facsimile services, and telephone calls. These expenses are not part of overhead and can be linked to specific clients. The rules allow lawyers to charge for them separately from attorneys' fees, but prohibit making a profit on them. They must be charged to the client at the firm's cost.

The seventh way that lawyers pad their bills is by excessively discussing cases among themselves. It's not uncommon for a junior lawyer to seek the advice of a senior lawyer on some aspect of a case and for both of them to bill the time that they spend together. This practice can cost the client dearly, because often the senior lawyer could perform the entire task in the time it takes to explain to the junior lawyer what to do. Ethical senior lawyers understand that young lawyers need training and will hold this sort of billing to a minimum. Others, however, are abusive, and you should review your statements to ensure that you are not a victim of such a practice.

The problem of lawyers conversing too much can occur between opposing lawyers as well, thus affecting clients on both sides. Once I represented the plaintiff in a personal injury lawsuit, and the lawyer for the defendant began to call me on a daily basis. At first, I thought that he was simply being diligent, but after a few days I noted that he was raising the same issues over and over again. The problem became so severe that I accused him of running up his client's bill by making worthless phone calls. He stopped calling, but I had not made a friend. My agreement with my client provided for fees that were contingent on the outcome of the case, so I had no incentive to waste time talking to another lawyer in order to increase the billing. When the fee agreements of both clients provide for hourly billing, however, the danger is ever present that the lawyers will talk to one another more than is necessary.

Even if you monitor your case closely, you will not be able to stop the padding of your bill completely. Most lawyers are determined, goal-oriented people, and some of them will bill those

10 to 14 hours every day come hell or high water. Otherwise, how can they become partners, earn yearly bonuses, and achieve their other professional goals? If you keep a log of your communications with your lawyer, insist upon detailed billings, and carefully review your monthly statements, you can substantially reduce the padding that is directed at you. Hopefully, the lawyer will then shift the padding to other clients or stop the practice altogether.

To combat padding, I suggest the following:

1. Ask your lawyer to produce monthly statements that specify the work performed and the time spent doing it. Insist that each activity be described with sufficient detail for you to understand precisely what was done. Request, as well, that each item in the statement carry its own time entry. Do not allow the lawyer to group activities together and bill only a total number of hours. (For more on billing statements, see Chapter 2.)

2. Ensure that the lawyer's time be recorded in tenth-hours rather than quarter hours. Make clear that short telephone calls are to be billed for no more than one tenth-hour.

3. Keep a log of your own conferences with your lawyer. Such a log is useful for cross-referencing with the monthly statements.

4. Insist that the lawyer bill only the actual time worked. For instance, ask if the lawyer charges a minimum time for being in court all day. Some lawyers charge 10 or 12 hours as a flat minimum while in trial, even if they are in court only 7 or 8 hours.

At the same time that you attend to the above details, however, you should try to be as fair as possible; otherwise, your lawyer may not be anxious to work hard on your behalf. But you should not allow yourself to become a cash cow for your lawyer. Do not hesitate to challenge your lawyer on work that appears to be invented or for which the time billed seems inflated. I have found that if I confront lawyers directly and state why the fee bothers me, they usually offer to make some reasonable adjustment.

2. Churning the Work

Some lawyers "churn" work in order to generate fees. The term is appropriate for referring to the filing of unnecessary motions, the writing of pointless legal briefs, and the creation of other superfluous work for the sole purpose of inflating attorneys' fees. Churning legal work differs from padding the bill. When churning, the lawyer actually works the number of hours billed. If it takes 1.5 hours to draft an unnecessary document, the lawyer charges the client 1.5 hours for the work. Of course, the lawyer may also pad the bill for work that has been churned, billing perhaps 2.0 hours for 1.5 hours spent in the preparation of a superfluous document.

The churning of work can include the repeated and often futile filing of motions with the court. A motion is a request that the judge rule on a specific issue. Lawyers sometimes file motions that have no chance of success in order to protect themselves against malpractice claims, like physicians who, just to be on the safe side, order patients to undergo unnecessary laboratory tests. You should thoroughly discuss with your lawyer the pros and cons of filing each motion and obtain a realistic assessment of the possibility of its being granted. Don't waste time and money on motions that have virtually no chance of success. Of course, if your lawyer has a good reason to file a motion with the court, follow the advice. You must use common sense.

Some of your lawyer's reasons for filing certain motions may surprise you. For instance, lawyers who understand that elected judges try to give something to the parties on both sides of a controversy often employ odd tactics. Elected judges are political beings. Much of what they do is aimed at not offending the public and at coercing lawyers to contribute funds to their political campaigns. Judges' rulings are often gutless compromises that carefully award something to each side, but afford real relief to no one. These politically driven decisions cause lawyers to do all sorts of strange things, including sometimes filing motions they know they will lose.

For example, if two motions must be granted for the client's position to be viable, the lawyer will perhaps file four of them, carefully crafting the two extra motions so that they appear to be legitimate, but knowing that they will be denied. The hope is that the judge will rule favorably on the two important motions, while ruling adversely on the frivolous ones. Thus, the lawyer gives the judge an opportunity to award something to both sides. The opposing lawyer, however, usually sees the ploy, and files several motions as well, also including a number of frivolous ones that will be denied.

This absurd spiral of feints and counter-feints costs you money and contributes to the overall delay of your case. You may not be able to avoid employing such tactics; your lawyer is simply working to keep your case alive in a messy system created by others. You need to be aware that these things go on, though, so you can recognize when such maneuvering is necessary and when your lawyer is churning the work to inflate the fees. There is no rule of thumb for determining when an activity is necessary and when it is not. You must be involved in every step of your case in order to know the difference.

3. The Good-Old-Boy Network

State judges are either elected or appointed (some states use a combination method), and their terms are limited in duration. Elected judges need campaign contributions to obtain and keep their positions. Appointed judges need friends and allies in order to receive and retain their appointments. The political agenda of the judge can cause a variety of political, social, economic, nepotistic, and other nonjudicial considerations to come into play in your case.

In some states where judges are elected by popular vote, lawyers are allowed to make contributions to judges' campaigns. In addition to giving actual campaign contributions, lawyers often extend assurances to judges that more money will be forthcoming should a serious opponent emerge in an upcoming election. As you might suspect, this twisted method of selecting judges often results in strange rulings and inconsistent judgments. Allowing contributions from lawyers to judges' campaigns perpetuates good-old-boy networks and contributes to unfair, inconsistent, and unpredictable outcomes in court.

Such systems continue in existence only because they benefit everyone in the chain of influence and power. Judges and lawyers feather each other's nests. The judges who receive campaign contributions benefit from high salaries and job security. The lawyers who make the contributions benefit from increased income derived from the slanted rulings of the judges. Many lawyers are happy to give money in exchange for four years of favorable rulings from a judge. The judges are content, because with support from the legal community and a formidable campaign fund, political opponents will hesitate to challenge them at election time.

Most judges are shrewd about how and when they rule in favor of friends or campaign contributors. If the issue presented clearly calls for a ruling in favor of a party whose lawyer is not a contributor to the judge's campaign, all but the most openly corrupt judges will rule for that party. On the close questions, however, judges can favor their friends and campaign contributors with impunity. Judges' allies win far more than their share of the close questions.

A few years ago, a law firm represented a corporation in a lawsuit against one of its former officers. Over the lawyers' objections, the judge decided to refer the case to a mediator to see if a settlement could be reached. The mediator, a local lawyer appointed by the judge, met with each side once and then held a joint meeting. He found the positions of the parties to be too far apart to reach a settlement and sent the case back to the court for continuation of the original proceedings.

The mediator spent no more than a total of ten hours on the case. In spite of that, the judge ordered the parties to pay the mediator a fee of thousands of dollars. Both parties considered the fee to be unfair, but there was a lot at stake in the case and no one wanted to upset the apple cart at that point, so each side paid its half.

The mediator received a windfall of far more than his services were worth. Come election time, how much do you suppose he gave to the judge's campaign? I can assure you that his contribution exceeded the price of a ticket to the judge's campaign fundraising party.

Another example of the operation of the good-old-boy network is that of judges appointing lawyers to represent children in settlement hearings or mentally ill persons in commitment proceedings and then awarding attorneys' fees for that service. In one instance, a well-connected lawyer received thousands of dollars for a representation that took only a few hours of his time. It's a safe bet that some portion of that money made its way back into the judge's campaign fund.

Examples abound, but you get the drift. The system of electing judges is riddled with problems that cannot be solved by enacting codes of professional conduct. Only removing the factors that motivate the conduct in the first place will solve them.

Lawyers' contributions to judges' political campaigns also make it difficult for honest lawyers to run for judicial office. One lawyer who was widely respected for his unwavering honesty and integrity was elected to the bench after a campaign strained by inadequate funding. Lawyers in the county generally liked him and thought he would be a good judge. They were reluctant to contribute money to his campaign, though, because they knew that he would make fair decisions no matter who supported him in the election. He was so honest that the lawyers foresaw no potential for returns on their investments.

4. Running up Your Opponent's Attorneys' Fees

An effective way to pressure opponents is to cause them to incur additional attorneys' fees and expenses. A party may do this in hopes that the opponent will not have the funds to proceed further or will be forced to cut corners on important portions of the case. A wealthy party can sometimes outspend the other party and eventually achieve a more favorable settlement than if both sides were evenly funded.

Financial pressure pushes cases toward settlement. With the passage of time, the parties begin to feel the strain on their pocketbooks, and settlement becomes more palatable to them. Plaintiffs sometimes have no money at all; they frequently rely on their lawyers to front expenses and to defer the payment of attorneys' fees until the end of the case. Lawyers may front expenses on a number of cases at once, so the pressure on them to settle some of them can be significant.

Generally speaking, initiating a court action is more expensive than responding to one. A few years ago, in a complicated commercial lawsuit, a lawyer represented the plaintiff on an hourly fee basis. After filing suit, he spent many hours poring over documents and drafting interrogatories and requests for admissions that were specific, clearly worded, and to the point. The defense lawyer objected to every question and admission, claiming that they were unclear and lacked specificity. The objections took him only a few minutes to draft. Not surprisingly, the judge did what judges do best — he floundered — and ruled that about half of the questions should be reworded. The objections forced the plaintiff's lawyer to attend a hearing and spend more time drafting new interrogatories, all of which cost his client additional money.

The defense lawyer won that round. He succeeded in causing the plaintiff to spend more money than his own client spent. The effect of such a spending difference is not always immediately apparent. The cumulative effect, however, of one side's constantly forcing the other to expend funds can be devastating. One of the measures of a good lawyer is the ability to oblige the other side to spend money. An artful lawyer is often able to cause the opposition to do extra work. If an imbalance in spending can be maintained for a prolonged period, the party who caused it often gains a substantial advantage in the case.

Judges frequently make middle-of-the-road rulings that work injustice on one party or the other. If you suspect that you are spending more than your opponent, encourage your lawyer to reverse that trend. If the spending discrepancy persists, you may decide to settle the case before you get dragged too far down the money hole.

5. Runaway Attorneys' Fees

Once you select a law firm, you may initially speak with a senior lawyer about your case. After the attorney-client agreement is executed, however, another lawyer, perhaps considerably less experienced, may be assigned to you. The law firm may enjoy a fine reputation in the community, but that does not mean that all of its lawyers are good ones. When you receive the news that your case has been reassigned, the senior lawyer may promise to oversee things and be available for consultation whenever necessary. The rhetoric sounds good, but as a practical matter, it is smoke blown at you to keep you happy. Once the junior lawyer takes over, you may never see the senior lawyer again. By the time you go to court, the senior lawyer will be so out of touch with your case as to be incapable of handling the trial.

What the senior lawyer hopes is that you will become comfortable working with the junior lawyer. In many instances, however, the quality of the work may be lower than it would have been had the senior lawyer handled the case. Furthermore, the notion that you save attorneys' fees by using a lawyer with a lower billing rate is mythical. Even though the junior lawyer's rate may be lower than that of the senior lawyer, the cost to you for the entire case will frequently be about the same as it would have been had the more experienced lawyer done the work. The inefficiencies of junior lawyers often increase the fees more than the amount saved through their lower billing rates.

The larger law firms have cores of senior lawyers who have proven their abilities not only to handle cases but also to manage their businesses. A law firm is a business. The senior lawyers ("partners" or "shareholders") hire a number of junior lawyers ("associates") and assign cases to them. The firm then establishes a billing policy that requires the associate lawyers to bill from 1,800 to 2,500 hours a year or more. Raises and bonuses are predicated largely on the number of hours that an associate bills and collects each year. Competition among associates is fierce, because only a few of them will be invited to become partners.

Law firms are structured as pyramids with ever-expanding bases. Small numbers of senior lawyers at the top take profits from the work of a greater number of associate lawyers below. Senior partners know that a top-heavy pyramid lowers profits for each of them, so few lawyers are allowed to enter that elite upper group.

All this creates a billing mentality in law firms that is costly to clients. An associate lawyer must bill more than seven hours every workday in order to accumulate 1,800 hours in one year. Working seven or eight hours per day is not difficult, but billing that many hours is another matter, and collecting the money is more difficult still. Time spent at firm meetings, talking to the secretary, or getting coffee should not be billed. Associate lawyers must be exceptionally well organized and self-disciplined if they are to record the hours necessary for a successful year. Typically, they spend 10 to 12 hours in the office each day to produce 7 hours of time that can be billed. If the firm's billing goal for associate lawyers is greater than 1,800 hours per year, then they must work even longer hours. This pressure to bill their clients forces associate lawyers to choose between having no life at all outside the law firm and finding creative ways to fabricate billing. A few of them sacrifice their personal lives for the sake of honest billing. The majority gets creative.

This billing mentality affects clients directly. Many lawyers bill for every second they remotely think about your case. If you are not diligent in monitoring the work and tracking the corresponding fees, you may join the ranks of clients who have paid for time spent at lunches, on the golf course, on the highway to and from work, and at social gatherings. It's difficult to avoid paying excessive attorneys' fees. At the hourly rates that lawyers charge, even legitimate billing is onerous for most clients. Your best bet is to be familiar with the work that's being done, who's doing it, and why it's necessary. If you turn your case over to your lawyer and ignore the details, chances are good that the fee will inflate, and the legal work that you receive will be no better than it would have been had you paid a more reasonable amount.

6. Wining and Dining

Expenses incurred by lawyers who are working on your case can soar out of control before you know it. Associate lawyers, recently graduated from law school, are often sent on out-of-town assignments that generate expenses. Sometimes these lawyers have never even met the clients, and their mindset becomes one of capitalizing on the perks instead of monitoring their spending as if the funds were their own. You can imagine the elaborate meals and other entertainment that have been charged to clients during such trips.

You should be on the lookout for other careless uses of your money as well. For instance, once a deposition of a witness has been taken, the court reporter makes a written transcript and delivers copies of it to the parties. You pay one fee for the time that the court reporter spends physically at the deposition, another for making the transcript, and yet another for the copies that are delivered to the parties. These fees are often high, so if you were to take the deposition of a potential witness and discover that the information contained in that testimony is not helpful to your case, you might not want to order a transcript. Sometimes you may want the transcript but with no extra copies, possibly because the court reporter's fee for copies is exorbitant.

You should be aware of how all of the players in the process make money. Maintaining a good relationship with the court reporter is important, so your lawyer may prefer to spend a little extra money on transcripts if the case will require further participation by the same person. But lawyers often become friendly with the court reporters, and they may purchase a transcript or have copies made more as a personal favor than out of necessity. These things require you to use common sense, but you can't do that if you don't know what's going on. Being involved with your case will allow you to make good decisions as the need arises.

7. Professional Courtesy

Professional courtesy is voluntary cooperation among lawyers that makes their jobs more friction free. It sometimes saves clients money, but frequently it is extended at their expense.

Opposing lawyers routinely reschedule events, extend deadlines, and exchange other courtesies without consulting their clients. If such changes create additional fees or expenses, the clients pay the price. At the same time, though, lawyers need authority to negotiate housekeeping matters so that the case can move along in an expeditious and orderly fashion. You should permit the rescheduling of hearings, depositions, and other meetings according to the reasonable needs of all the participants. When the rescheduling becomes excessive, though, and you suspect that some of it may be to facilitate activities like a Friday afternoon round of golf, you may want to insist that you be notified in advance of any postponements or cancellations. If you are watching your case closely, you will know what is reasonable and what is excessive.

A small minority of lawyers who already dislike each other costs their clients money by refusing to cooperate with one another. Feuds between lawyers are not uncommon, and they can be expensive propositions for their clients. A contentious lawyer may, for example, refuse to agree to a reasonable date or time for a deposition. This forces the opposing lawyer to file a motion, attend a hearing, and ask the judge to set the date and time. Judges routinely grant such requests, so it's in the best interests of all involved to come to an agreement without resorting to a hearing. If such conflicts emerge in your case, you should not try to squelch them entirely (anything that puts your lawyer in a fighting mood can't be all bad), but you should instruct your lawyer to cooperate at least to a degree that does not cost you money unnecessarily.

Professional courtesy has a proper place in every case. If extended responsibly, it facilitates the smooth passage of your case through the pretrial stages. But do not let it cause excessive delay. If you stay closely involved with your case, you should be able to recognize abuses of professional courtesy and prevent them.

CHAPTER 5

THE TRIAL

In Chapter 3 you learned how to monitor your lawyer's activities from the initial consultation through the trial. You will find it helpful, as well, to know something about the trial itself so that you understand the final goal toward which you and your lawyer will be working. The following explanation is not to be used as a guide for trying your own lawsuit.[1] Rather, it is an orientation that is intended to help you make better decisions with your lawyer immediately before and during your trial.

This chapter begins by describing three of the salient qualities of a good trial lawyer. The first two — experience and toughness — are discussed in Chapter 1 along with other factors to consider when selecting a lawyer. A lawyer's preparedness for hearings and trial is difficult to ascertain at the outset of the attorney-client relationship. That is why it is not addressed in Chapter 1. Experience, toughness, and preparedness are all examined in this chapter. Their presence or absence in your lawyer's war chest of qualities will unfold as your case proceeds.

---

1. Situations in which you might consider self-representation are rare. Generally speaking, if you are a party to litigation, you need a lawyer.

The remainder of the chapter tracks a typical jury trial from the filing of pretrial motions to the rendering of a verdict and ends with a brief discussion of the courts. No matter what your jurisdiction, this overview should generally apprise you of the obstacles that you are likely to encounter at trial. The procedures in your locale may vary from the details set forth here.

1. Qualities of a Trial Lawyer

You should look for three qualities — experience, toughness, and preparedness — in a good trial lawyer:

1.1 Experience

Do not allow your case to become the training ground for a lawyer who needs courtroom experience. You are under no obligation to help anyone begin a career in law. If you go into a trial with an under-gunned lawyer, you run the risk of achieving a disappointing result. Lawyers and judges employ hundreds of little tricks at trial, not all of which are clean and aboveboard, as you may well imagine. The courtroom is like a poker game — the object is to win, and some of the players go to great lengths to accomplish that end. Fair Play, Justice, and Integrity often fold as the game proceeds. At trial, you may get shot at from under the table or belatedly discover that the deck is stacked against you. A novice is at an extreme disadvantage there.

Many courtroom deceptions are subtle and go entirely unnoticed by inexperienced lawyers. Some lawyers are so naive that they deny that the chicanery really happens. If you and your lawyer are both new at the trial game, you will almost certainly get fooled, and you may never even know it.

When I was a prosecutor, I tried a felony case against a new lawyer. The offense was drug-related, and the lawyer made no objection to the first five exhibits — drugs and paraphernalia — that I offered into evidence. Something in the tone of his voice each time he said, "No objection, Your Honor," led me to suspect that he did not know how disruptive a few objections could have been to my case. The rules required me to establish lengthy proofs of chain of custody and to present other foundational testimony before admission would be proper. I decided to take a chance, and I offered exhibits 6 through 53 into evidence all at the same time. Even though the judge raised his eyebrows and increased the volume of his voice as he asked for objections, the young lawyer again stood up and said, "No objection, Your Honor." Aside from implicitly admitting (by his failure to object) that the items offered as exhibits were in his client's apartment, he saved me hours of time at trial. If he had made the proper objections, it would have taken me all day to get that evidence admitted, and I was elated to find the job done by 9:30 a.m.

One device that is often used in trial and that is difficult for neophyte lawyers to recognize and counter, is the speaking objection. A speaking objection is either an improper objection that illustrates a point to the jury that the lawyer could not otherwise make, or a proper one to which the lawyer attaches extra verbiage, making an additional point that is impermissible. The more brazen lawyers will say nearly anything in an objection, and often, unless the opposing lawyer objects to the extra commentary, the judge will do nothing about it. If a speaking objection is clearly out of order, the judge may put a stop to the lawyer's shenanigans. Speaking objections are commonplace in trials in which one lawyer is experienced and the other is not. The verbal damage that a good trial lawyer can do to a green lawyer is extensive. A veteran trial lawyer is much more hesitant to add improper language in the presence of a seasoned opponent.

The judge can also deceive your lawyer. Judges detest having their decisions reversed on appeal by appellate courts. Such reversals offend their egos, embarrass them before their colleagues, and in states where judges are elected, damage their reputations with voters. Political aspirants seeking judicial office frequently cite the records of incumbent trial judges who have suffered repeated reversals of their decisions by appellate courts. The implication is that they do not follow the law or do not know which law to follow. In order for lawyers to use their objections to the adverse rulings of judges effectively, the objections must be properly preserved.[2] As a consequence, judges sometimes do strange

2. Certain portions of the testimony, motions to the court, and objections must be recorded by the court reporter before a judge's decision can be appealed and reversed.

things at trial to keep the lawyers off balance. A cantankerous judge can fail to rule on an objection or cause a lawyer to omit critical objections or motions, leaving the record incomplete and perhaps useless for appeal purposes.

I know of one judge who makes a habit of telling his court reporter to stop recording whenever possible so that much of what the lawyers say is lost. The court reporter works for the judge and always follows the judge's instructions. It takes a strong-willed, seasoned trial lawyer to stand up to a bully judge and insist upon making a complete record to preserve objections. Experienced trial lawyers know which judges play what tricks, when tough action is necessary, and when to let the judges play their little games.

If your case is to be presented to a jury, look for a lawyer who has completed at least 15 jury trials. These trials should have been taken all the way to judgment, uninterrupted by directed verdicts,[3] mistrials,[4] or settlements. Fifteen is not too much to ask. Over the course of a career, an active civil trial lawyer may try in excess of 50 cases before juries. For criminal lawyers, the number is higher.

1.2 Toughness

Trial is combative. It functions like a war waged according to rules that allow the combatants to fight without taking the law into their own hands. To the extent that individuals settle their differences in the courts, personal revenge has become civilized. Even so, a trial is a form of conflict; like warfare itself, it is a messy matter.

To engage effectively in such hostilities, you need a warrior (your lawyer) who is tough and combat-ready to fight for you. The tax lawyer who saved you money when you were audited last year probably has not developed the adeptness at trial or the obdurate personality required to represent you competently in court. Only a seasoned trial lawyer will have the skill and intestinal fortitude

---

3. A directed verdict is one in which the judge instructs the jury to return a specific verdict because the evidence is so compelling that only one decision is reasonable.

4. A mistrial is a trial that the judge stops in midstream because of a procedural error, serious misconduct on the part of a party, lawyer, or juror, or the jury's inability to agree on a verdict.

to do battle with the judge, the opposing lawyer, and the shifty witnesses who lie under oath.

1.3 Preparedness

Any case can be made stronger through good preparation. As you approach the trial date, your lawyer should begin to prepare witnesses, organize documents, and plan the trial presentation. If this does not happen, you should do some prodding. Many lawyers wait until the last minute to get ready, largely because most cases settle before trial. Do not let your lawyer get away with that. Well-prepared cases frequently settle more favorably than poorly prepared ones.

Some lawyers show up on the day of the trial and try to wing it. Even the simplest of trials is too complex to improvise, no matter how gifted the lawyer may be. When lawyers ad-lib, they nearly always forget something important — a question they should have asked, a motion they should have made, a point they should have emphasized. The only way to run a perfect trial is to prepare.

As soon as you receive a firm trial date, ask your lawyer to show you a plan for the final preparation. A few weeks before your trial, you should meet with your lawyer to discuss the testimony that will be presented. In a civil proceeding, the depositions of opposing witnesses should already have been taken and all documents and physical evidence should have been gathered by this time. During the final days before your trial, you and your lawyer must select the testimonial, physical, and documentary evidence that you want to present, decide upon the order of presentation, and plan each phase such that the whole thing comes out like a well-directed drama. The timing of these meetings with your lawyer will vary depending upon the court, the size of the case, and the number of witnesses.

I prefer to work with lawyers who write out the questions that they plan to ask their witnesses. This allows me to discuss the questions with the lawyer and suggest additional ones. Your lawyer should interview each witness carefully so that there are no surprises at trial. Nothing is more embarrassing than examining your own witness and receiving a reply that you did not anticipate. Such surprises, even on minor details, can cause a jury to stray from the central issues for deliberation. Unexpected answers rarely help your cause. Thorough preparation will reduce the number of unanticipated responses to a minimum.

Although you should be aware of your lawyer's process for creating questions, you should avoid micromanaging your lawyer's efforts. If you see that the preparation of witnesses is moving forward in an orderly fashion, let your lawyer do the job. The rules give your lawyer the final say-so on tactical matters, and you must learn to strike a balance between observation and intervention in your case.

Some lawyers use trial notebooks to organize their presentations for trial, but file folders or other organizational systems work just as well. The trial notebook is usually divided into sections according to the anticipated order of presentation at trial and contains only the portions to be delivered by your lawyer. Sample 3 shows how the sections of a notebook for a civil trial might be labeled.

The pleadings, answers to interrogatories, and deposition transcripts will probably be filed elsewhere; excerpts from them or references to them may appear in the trial notebook. Some lawyers keep all the documents that will be offered into evidence in a single folder. I prefer to place them in the folders of the witnesses who will be used to introduce them. In addition, I maintain a list of exhibits on the table before me and mark each one as it is either admitted into or excluded from the evidence. I also keep a detailed list of the order of trial and check off each step as it is completed. Every lawyer has a different style of organization and preparation. It does not matter what method is used as long as it functions effectively in making an orderly trial presentation.

If you monitor the development of your case, adequate preparation by your lawyer should not be a problem. Make clear at the initial interview that you expect thorough preparation for every hearing and for trial, and get a commitment from your lawyer to do such preparation. Then follow your case closely enough to ensure that your lawyer lives up to that agreement.

SAMPLE 3
TRIAL NOTEBOOK SECTIONS

- Pretrial Motions
- Jury Selection
- Opening Statement
- Plaintiff's Testimony
- Plaintiff's Witness 1
- Plaintiff's Witness 2
- Plaintiff's Expert Witness
- Motions
- Defendant's Testimony
- Defendant's Witness 1
- Defendant's Witness 2
- Defendant's Expert Witness
- Jury Instructions*
- Closing Argument
- Law, Research, Anticipated Objections
- Exhibit List
- Checklists

---

*In federal court and some state courts, the judge reads the jury instructions to the jury after the lawyers have made their closing arguments.

2. Basic Elements of a Trial

A jury trial is essentially the same in format and appearance in both state and federal court. Some important differences do exist, but for the purposes of this overview, we can consider them to be the same. The goal here is not to turn you into a trial lawyer but rather to give you an elementary understanding of what to expect at trial. The terminology used for the different phases of the trial and for the activities that take place there may vary from jurisdiction to jurisdiction. You will have to adapt the information that you glean from these pages to your specific situation.

Judges frequently schedule several trials to begin on the same day. They do so to force cases to settle, move their trial schedules forward, and ensure that there will always be a case for the jurors to hear. If, for instance, your case is number four on the judge's list of trials set to start on a given day, your trial will be postponed if one of the three cases ahead of yours goes to trial. If all three cases settle or are postponed, then yours moves to the top of the list and your jury selection starts that day.

No matter whether you are the plaintiff or the defendant, you are not likely to forget your first day at trial. You will be nervous, especially if you have not spent much time in a courtroom, and you will observe lots of mysterious goings on. If you have diligently studied your case, you will understand the facts that your lawyer will present, and you will have some idea about the nature of the opposition's evidence. After reading this chapter, you should understand the basic trial format. Your familiarity with the order of the proceedings will allow you to concentrate on the important aspects of your case.

Trying a case requires your lawyer to focus on the matters at hand, and it will help if you focus on them as well. You should avoid, for example, whispering thoughts about your own testimony to your lawyer during the testimony of a witness. Unless your comment has to do with the activity of the moment, wait for a break to make it. Keep paper and pencil handy for taking notes regarding the testimony and for writing suggestions to your lawyer. Your lawyer will appreciate your attending to the concerns immediately before you.

When you enter the courthouse on the morning of trial, you will see people in the courtroom and in the hallway outside. The opposing lawyer and your opponent will probably be there, along with jurors, bailiff, court reporter, and others. You should always stay as far away from these people as possible without giving them the impression that you are avoiding them. The less you talk to them, or to other people while within earshot of them, the better.

Anything your opponents hear you say could potentially be used against you at your trial. All the opposing lawyer has to do is call you to the witness stand and ask you to repeat what you said in the hallway before the trial or on a break. If you said something like, "I only sued her because my doctor said I should," to a friend in the coffee shop, you could be asked about the comment. Your friend might even be called to testify regarding the remark. If you are suing based on a physical injury, as in an automobile accident, the jury might infer from the comment that you were not as severely injured as you claim or that you are not all that interested in the case. The opposing lawyer will almost certainly characterize it that way.

So be quiet. Talk about your case with no one but your lawyer and only when no one else can hear you. While conversing with friends or family during breaks, try not to discuss the trial. If you must do so, make absolutely certain that no one else is nearby. Many subtle conclusions can be drawn from your actions in and around the courthouse. Watch what you do and say at all times.

You also should be conscious of your demeanor inside the courtroom. The facial expression that you maintain in trial should be that of a good poker player, showing no emotion either way as the testimony proceeds. Keep your head up and listen intently to each witness as if nothing surprises or affects you. It probably does no harm to look concerned. Most jurors can understand why you might be worried at trial, and they will not take it to mean that you are in the wrong. You must be careful, though, because emotional responses to testimony can alienate a juror. Some jurors make their decisions based solely on their impressions of the parties rather than on the evidence presented.

Sample 4 is an example of the order of events in a jury trial. The order of events in your own trial should proceed approximately as shown. Specific terminology used to describe the different phases of the proceeding may vary with the jurisdiction. The number of witnesses and the order of their testimonies will vary depending on the facts of the case and the strategies adopted by the lawyers. For criminal trials, you can substitute "prosecutor" wherever "plaintiff" appears, and the order will be substantially the same, except that the defendant will rarely testify. In federal court and some state courts, the lawyers make their closing arguments before the judge reads the instructions to the jury. Each portion of the trial is explained briefly in the sections following Sample 4.

SAMPLE 4
SAMPLE ORDER OF A TRIAL

- Pretrial Motions
- Jury Selection
- Plaintiff's Opening Statement
- Defendant's Opening Statement (The defendant normally has the option of presenting the opening statement here or at the beginning of the defendant's case.)
- Plaintiff's Case Begins
  - Plaintiff's Testimony
  - Plaintiff's Witness 1
  - Plaintiff's Witness 2
  - Plaintiff's Expert Witness
- Plaintiff Rests (This marks the end of the plaintiff's initial presentation of evidence. Certain proof must be made before resting if the case is to survive the upcoming motions.)
- Motions
- Defendant's Case Begins
  - Defendant's Testimony (Sometimes the plaintiff's lawyer will call the defendant to testify during the plaintiff's case. In that event, the defendant's lawyer may decide not to call the defendant again during the defendant's presentation. Defendants in criminal cases usually do not testify.)
  - Defendant's Witness 1
  - Defendant's Witness 2
  - Defendant's Expert Witness

- Defendant Rests
- Plaintiff May Have a Right to Call Rebuttal Witnesses
- Defendant May Have a Right to Call Surrebuttal* Witnesses
- Plaintiff Closes (This marks the end of all evidence to be presented by the party who closes.)
- Defendant Closes
- Requests for Jury Instructions (This is done outside the presence of the jury.)
- Judge Prepares Jury Instructions (This is done outside the presence of the jury.)
- Judge Reads Instructions to the Jury (In federal court and some state courts, the judge reads the jury instructions after the lawyers make their closing arguments.)
- Plaintiff's Closing Argument — First Portion
- Defendant's Closing Argument
- Plaintiff's Closing Argument — Final Portion
- Jury Deliberations
- Jury Verdict

*A surrebuttal is a response to a rebuttal.

2.1 Pretrial motions

Before the jury panel is brought into the courtroom for jury selection, the lawyers will have an opportunity to present some last-minute motions to the judge. These motions can be presented either verbally or in writing, but important ones are nearly always submitted in writing.

Pretrial motions are extremely important. You should discuss them with your lawyer before the trial so you understand the impact that the judge's granting or denying them will have on your case. Certain motions can restrain an opposing lawyer who habitually blurts out damaging comments or intentionally elicits improper testimony. If your lawyer anticipates an inappropriate comment, and the judge grants a motion excluding that language, then the opposing lawyer is prohibited from making the comment and risks a reprimand from the judge or even a mistrial if the prohibition is not respected.

2.2 Jury selection

As the trial begins, a panel of approximately 50 potential jurors files into the courtroom and takes seats assigned to them by a clerk or bailiff. The judge enters the courtroom, and the lawyers are then allowed to question the panel as part of the jury-selection process called the *voir dire*.[5] The *voir dire* is an examination of prospective jurors to determine whether or not they are qualified to serve on the jury. It is the only time during the trial when the lawyers are allowed to talk directly with the jurors.[6] The dialogue created in this phase of the proceeding is often lively and informative. The inquiry is supposed to be strictly limited to determining if the jurors harbor biases or prejudices that make them unfit to sit as jurors in that particular case. Many lawyers are artful, however, at introducing all sorts of facts, laws, opinions, and arguments in their *voir dire* presentations. Lawyers who are skilled in the art of *voir dire* examination can advance their clients' causes greatly during this question and answer period.

Challenges of jurors are called "strikes." A final jury is selected from the panel by striking (eliminating from the list) the disqualified or unwanted jurors' names from the list. The resulting jurors make up the jury that will hear the case.

During the selection process, each side has an opportunity to challenge an unlimited number of jurors based on actual biases or prejudices demonstrated through their answers. These are called "challenges for cause." The judge rules on each challenge and excuses individuals who demonstrate biases that make them

---

5. Pronounced "vwär dir."

6. In state court, your lawyer is allowed to question the jurors directly. In federal court, the judge usually asks the questions.

inappropriate jurors for the case. Any number of jurors can be struck for cause.

Each side can also strike a fixed number of jurors, usually three to ten, depending upon the type of case and the jurisdiction. These are called "peremptory challenges" (or peremptory strikes), and the parties can make them for any reason or for no reason at all. They cannot, however, eliminate a juror solely on the basis of race. In spite of this rule, lawyers typically strike jurors according to any whim they have in their heads at the time. Discovering the reasons behind those decisions is extremely difficult.

When the panel of prospective jurors files into the courtroom, the judge, the lawyers, and the parties are already in their places. The clerk assigns seats to the members of the panel in numerical order. Sometimes the seating assignments are not made until the morning of the trial, so your lawyer may not know in advance where a juror's name will fall on the list. A few minutes before the panel enters, each lawyer receives a list of the jurors' names arranged in the same numerical order as their seating assignments. In some jurisdictions, the jurors report for duty the week before the trial. At that time, each panel member fills out a personal data sheet. Some courts provide copies of these personal data sheets to the lawyers well in advance of the trial. Others make it a last-minute affair. Receiving such information beforehand is helpful, because the time allotted to each side for asking questions of the panel is usually limited, and the time allowed afterward for deciding which jurors to eliminate from the list is quite short.

Sample 5 is a diagram of how the challenges work. Once the strikes are made, the first 12 panelists who are not eliminated make up the final jury. The illustration assumes that each side is allowed ten peremptory challenges.

SAMPLE 5
DIAGRAM OF CHALLENGES

PLAINTIFF'S CHALLENGES	PANEL MEMBERS	DEFENDANT'S CHALLENGES
	~~1~~	Challenge for cause
	~~2~~	Peremptory challenge #1
	3 (Juror #1)	
	4 (Juror #2)	
Challenge for cause	~~5~~	
Peremptory challenge #1	~~6~~	
	~~7~~	Peremptory challenge #2
	8 (Juror #3)	
	9 (Juror #4)	
	~~10~~	Peremptory challenge #3
Peremptory challenge #2	~~11~~	
Peremptory challenge #3	~~12~~	
Peremptory challenge #4	~~13~~	
	~~14~~	Peremptory challenge #4
	15 (Juror #5)	
	16 (Juror #6)	
	~~17~~	Challenge for cause
	~~18~~	Peremptory challenge #5
Peremptory challenge #5	~~19~~	
Peremptory challenge #6	~~20~~	
	21 (Juror #7)	
	~~22~~	Peremptory challenge #6
	~~23~~	Peremptory challenge #7
	24 (Juror #8)	
	25 (Juror #9)	
Peremptory challenge #7	~~26~~	

Peremptory challenge #8	27	
	28	Challenge for cause
	29	Peremptory challenge #8
	30 (Juror #10)	
Peremptory challenge #9	31	
Peremptory challenge #10	32	
	33 (Juror #11)	
	34	Peremptory challenge #9
	35	Peremptory challenge #10
	36 (Juror #12)	
	37-50 Not reached in selection process	

From the example, you can see that the first 12 jurors who are not crossed off the list are those numbered 3, 4, 8, 9, 15, 16, 21, 24, 25, 30, 33, and 36 (marked in parentheses in the center column as Jurors #1 – #12). These jurors will make up the final jury that will sit for the case. You know that the lawyers have done a good job when their strikes, which are done in secret, do not conflict. When both lawyers use a peremptory strike to eliminate the same juror, it is called a "double strike." Double striking is a waste of valuable peremptory challenges. Two experienced trial lawyers will rarely double their strikes on more than one juror.[7]

In some jurisdictions, each party has a right to one shuffle of the jury panel. A shuffle is a random reordering of jurors much like shuffling a deck of cards. If several of the jurors near the top of the list appear to be undesirable, the lawyer can ask that the list be shuffled into a new numerical order. Potentially, the judge could present three different lists of prospective jurors (an initial one and a shuffled one for each party), each with the names in a different order, before the jury panel is brought into the courtroom.

---

7. In some jurisdictions, double striking is impossible because the lawyers take turns making their strikes on the same list.

For example, if five or six potential jurors that one lawyer considers undesirable appear toward the top of the list, forcing the use of too many peremptory challenges, the lawyer may decide to request a shuffle. The shuffle repositions the jurors into new numerical positions, and the requesting lawyer's hope is that some of the unwanted jurors will fall to the bottom of the list, where they will be unlikely to become part of the sitting jury. This repositioning allows the lawyer to make better use of peremptory strikes.

2.2a Questions to consider

The questions that the lawyers ask of the panel during jury selection vary from case to case. Below is information that might be helpful in designing your questions. You may disagree with some of the conclusions as to how certain jurors might tend to vote, but in any event, this list should give you some ideas regarding how to create the questions.

- *Friendships and acquaintances.* Prudent lawyers will ask whether the prospective juror is personally acquainted with the parties, judge, bailiff, court reporter, lawyers, witnesses, or other jurors. Personal relationships can sway a juror's vote. The selection of jurors with such relationships may be impossible to avoid in rural settings.

- *Age.* Young people may tend to be lenient toward criminal defendants. Older people may be willing to help out someone with a work-related injury but intolerant of someone accused of robbery.

- *Gender.* Women may sympathize with the wife in a divorce case. Men may understand why someone gets into a fight in a bar. Either may be outraged by a violent rape, but women might be more empathetic than men regarding a female who has been battered by her boyfriend.

- *Served on prior juries.* As a defendant in a complicated commercial lawsuit, you may desire a seasoned juror to be the presiding juror. As a defendant in a criminal matter, you may want jurors who have never served before.

- *Prior injuries.* As a plaintiff, you may prefer a juror who has suffered an injury similar to yours. Conversely, you may want to avoid such a juror if you are the defendant.

- *Mothers Against Drunk Drivers (MADD).* Prosecutors prefer these people when intoxication is part of the case. In appropriate circumstances, you should ask not only which panelists are members of MADD, but also which ones sympathize with the objectives of that organization.

- *National Rifle Association (NRA).* In a prosecution for illegal possession of a firearm, both sides will want to know which prospective jurors are members of or sympathizers with the NRA.

- *Belief in and willingness to follow the law.* A juror's opinion about the controlling law of the case may cause you to choose or eliminate that person.

- *Victim of crime.* Has the prospective juror been a victim of a burglary, robbery, or other crime? Such traumatic experiences can greatly affect the prospective juror's attitude in a criminal case, even if the offense is nonviolent.

- *Race and nationality.* Race is not a proper criterion for eliminating jurors. Your lawyer can, however, appropriately ask if the race of one of the parties would affect the juror's ability to make a fair and impartial decision. In some parts of the country, prospective jurors are asked if they would be biased against aliens accused of a crime.

- *Profession.* Jurors' professions may reveal something about their attitudes toward certain issues. A laborer may understand someone's pain and suffering from a back injury or the emotional condition of a worker who is laid off by an employer. Professors and teachers tend to be liberal and may be inclined to award probation in criminal cases. Computer programmers may be desirable jurors for technical civil cases filled with details and complicated facts. Jurors' friendships or family connections with law enforcement officers, lawyers, accountants, physicians, or insurance agents may also affect their opinions regarding some topics.

These are only some ideas regarding information that your lawyer may wish to obtain from the jury panel. The questions that your lawyer decides to ask may be different from the ones suggested above. Before the trial, ask your lawyer what criteria should be used for jury selection in your case. Then discuss the formulation of questions to be directed to the panel. You should make your own suggestions regarding the questions you want to ask and the kinds of people you would like to have on your jury. An added benefit of this dialogue is that it will help stimulate your lawyer to think about all aspects of the trial.

Good lawyers set up their cases during the *voir dire* examination. Although it is a time for gathering information about the jurors, it is also an opportunity to teach them about the case. When a lawyer uses the jury selection to the fullest extent permitted under the rules, the trial may be practically won before the first witness is called to testify.

2.3   Opening statement

The opening statement is a summary of the facts that a party intends to prove during the trial. Both lawyers usually present their opening statements immediately before the plaintiff's case. Their remarks give the jury a preview of what they believe the evidence will show. The defendant's lawyer has the option of delivering the opening statement immediately following the plaintiff's opening or at the beginning of the defendant's case. Most defendants choose to give their opening statements at the beginning of the trial.

Lawyers generally agree that the opening statement can make a big difference in the outcome of the case. Studies show that jury verdicts are often consistent with the initial impressions of jurors after listening to the opening statements. A trial is similar to a classroom — the lawyer who does the most effective job of teaching the jury usually comes out ahead.

The irony regarding the opening statement is that although most lawyers believe it to be important, few use it effectively. It may be the part of the trial most overlooked by lawyers. Many of them take only a few minutes to deliver their opening statements, and the use of diagrams and other visual aids is the exception rather than the rule. Judges have become accustomed to lawyers' sloppy practices. In many instances, the opening statement is nothing more than a boring interlude between the jury selection and the first witness's testimony.

In some states, the opening statement has been replaced, in part, by the *voir dire* examination. Judges in those jurisdictions give so much latitude to lawyers to describe hypothetical facts and discuss the law during the jury selection that much of the function of the opening statement is usurped at that time. The opening statements of run-of-the-mill trials become simple summaries of what the facts will show, with little embellishment or theatrics to go with them.

The opening statement is supposed to be limited to a straightforward declaration of what the party intends to prove at trial. Argument is inappropriate at this stage and is reserved for the end of the trial when all the evidence has been presented. In courts with weak judges, however, the lawyers sometimes argue their cases during the opening statements.

The opening statement should be concise and to the point, leaving no doubt about what the evidence will show. Most lawyers are not nearly so creative with opening statements as the rules allow them to be. Talk to your lawyer about the opening statement and suggest making a major production of it. For cases in which a lot is at stake, a good opening statement can pay great dividends.

2.4 Plaintiff's case

The plaintiff's case consists principally of oral testimony presented through a series of witnesses. Photographs and diagrams can become part of a witness's testimony and are particularly useful for explaining processes and scenes. Most documents are introduced into evidence through witnesses' testimonies. Lawyers may also use witnesses to read deposition testimony to the jury. The evidence typically includes oral testimony, documents, physical objects, photographs, or diagrams, all introduced through witnesses.

The order of witnesses presented at trial will vary depending on the story that the plaintiff's lawyer wants to tell. Some lawyers start off with the plaintiff's testimony in order to throw their best punch right away. Others prefer to save the best for last, hoping in that way to hold the jurors' interest throughout the testimonies of the plaintiff's other witnesses. If there is expert testimony, and the expert is expensive, that may partially dictate the order of witnesses. A plaintiff will not want a physician who is billing $2,500 per hour (and complaining about losing money at that rate) to wait outside the courtroom for very long.

Some plaintiffs' lawyers like to call the defendant as their first witness just to catch the defense off guard. Defense lawyers sometimes forget to warn their clients of this possibility. Being forced to testify earlier than expected rattles some defendants and makes defense lawyers nervous, too. If you are a defendant, you should be prepared to give your testimony during the plaintiff's case if you are called to do so.

At this point, the plaintiff rests, which means that the plaintiff has no more evidence to present at this stage of the trial.

2.5 Motions

Once the plaintiff's lawyer has completed the presentation of the initial evidence and has rested, the judge will consider any motions that apply to the evidence heard up to that point. These motions are made outside of the presence of the jury. The most common motion to be presented is the defendant's motion for a directed verdict. This motion alleges that the threshold proof requirements of the plaintiff's case have not been met. If the judge agrees, the case could end here in favor of the defendant.

2.6 Defendant's case

The defense lawyer then begins, and the order of witnesses for the defendant's case is just as difficult to predict as it was for the plaintiff's. The defendant's lawyer may or may not call the defendant to testify, depending on whether the defendant testified earlier. If the plaintiff called the defendant to testify during the plaintiff's case, the defense lawyer may not want to give the plaintiff's lawyer another shot at questioning the defendant.

In criminal cases, defendants rarely take the witness stand. The burden to prove the guilt of the accused rests with the prosecution, and the accused is technically presumed to be innocent. Typically, the defendant asserts the right not to testify and remains silent throughout the trial. The judge instructs the jury not to consider the defendant's silence as an indicator of guilt, but many jurors do so anyway, in spite of the instruction. In some cases, convincing 12 jurors that the defendant is not guilty without presenting the defendant's testimony is exceedingly difficult. Most of the criminal defendants for whom I have obtained jury verdicts of not guilty have testified at their trials. Without their testimonies, I am absolutely certain they would have been found guilty. Such testimonies are precarious undertakings, however, and must be approached with the utmost solicitude. Many examples exist of silent defendants who have been found not guilty. In any event, criminal defense lawyers are uniformly cautious when it comes to the presentation of the defendant's testimony.

At this point, the defendant rests, which means that the defense has no more evidence to present at this time.

2.7 Jury instructions

Once all of the evidence has been presented for both sides and any rebuttal testimony has been given, the lawyers close. To execute this, they stand in turn and say to the judge, "The plaintiff (or defendant) closes, Your Honor." Those simple statements mark the completion of the presentation of evidence and indicate that the lawyers are ready to make their closing arguments. The jury is sent to the jury room, and the lawyers have an opportunity to request specific jury instructions. The judge rules on those requests, and the judge's assistant produces final copies of the instructions for each lawyer, the judge, and in state court, the jury. Then the lawyers record their objections to any instructions that they feel are inappropriate or unjustified by the law or the evidence that was presented.

Once the jury instructions are ready, the jury returns to the courtroom, and the judge reads the instructions to them word for word. The document is usually several pages long, so the reading can take five to ten minutes or even longer. In state court, the bailiff gives a copy of the instructions to the jury when they retire for their deliberations.

2.8   Closing arguments

After the instructions have been read to the jury, the lawyers are allowed to make their closing arguments. The plaintiff's lawyer argues twice, and the defendant's once. The rules permit the plaintiff's lawyer (or the prosecutor in criminal cases) to argue first and last, because the burden of proof[8] is on the plaintiff to substantiate the elements of the cause of action. Most judges, however, set a time limit for the argument, so the plaintiff's lawyer must be careful not to use too much time on the first portion of the closing argument. Plaintiffs' lawyers (and prosecutors in criminal cases) usually reserve as much time as possible for the final portion in order to rebut the arguments of the defendant. In some states, the time reserved for the final portion can be no greater than one-half of the total time allowed for the closing argument.

In constructing the closing argument, the plaintiff's lawyer must decide how to apportion the allotted time between the first and final segments of the argument. On one hand, the plaintiff's lawyer would like to say as little as possible in the first portion of the argument that could provide ammunition for the defendant's closing remarks. On the other, the plaintiff's lawyer must cover all important points at least briefly in the first portion of the closing argument, because the defendant could conceivably waive closing argument and prevent the plaintiff from arguing again.

The better plaintiff's lawyers usually say little in the first portion of the closing argument that can be refuted. They typically address the jury on organizational matters, thank them for their service, make a cursory statement that the elements of the cause of action have been fulfilled, and then sit down. The tactical goal

---

8. The burden of proof is a party's duty to present evidence supporting an assertion or charge.

of the plaintiff's lawyer in the first portion of the argument is to take command of the courtroom and appear to be running the show while saying as little as possible. One approach is to explain to the jury how the jury instructions should be used in their deliberations, briefly review the elements set out in the instructions, and make perfunctory statements regarding how the evidence fulfills each of them. Another approach, a more daring one, is to use some of the time to anticipate and rebut in advance the defense's best arguments. In any event, the plaintiff's strongest points are best left for the final portion of the closing argument, when the defendant has no further opportunity to respond.

2.9 Jury deliberations

Once the lawyers have finished their arguments, the jurors retire to the jury room to deliberate. They usually take a short break so they can stretch their legs, use the rest rooms, or fill their coffee mugs. Once everyone is settled, they choose a presiding juror. The selection sometimes takes a few minutes, not because it is difficult but rather because at this point no one is in charge.

Good juries follow the judge's instructions to the letter. In addition to protocol and housekeeping matters, the instructions include a list of elements that the plaintiff (or prosecution in criminal cases) must prove in order to prevail. The jury should focus on deciding whether evidence has been presented regarding each element and whether that evidence meets the standard of proof required in the instructions. Generally, in civil cases each element must be proved by a preponderance of the evidence; in criminal cases each one must be proved beyond a reasonable doubt.

Lawyers go to great lengths to explain the preponderance and reasonable doubt standards of proof in their *voir dire* presentations, opening statements, and closing arguments. The definitions and illustrations that judges permit vary with the rules and practices of each jurisdiction, but defining these terms is always a struggle. Lawyers are often not completely sure what preponderance and reasonable doubt really mean, and the contorted distinctions they attempt to draw are lost on many jurors. Most jurors create their own standard. They listen to the evidence, determine whom to believe or not believe, and then decide what to do. The beauty of it is that most of the time they make reasonable decisions.

2.10 Awaiting the verdict

The only thing left to do is wait. If the judge believes the verdict could be quick, the lawyers and parties will be told not to leave the courthouse. If the verdict could take longer, everyone is excused and asked to provide a telephone number where they can be reached.

As you wait for a verdict at the courthouse, you should be careful not to talk within hearing distance of the opposition. An unwise statement may provoke a motion to reopen the evidence or could be used against you in a second trial in the event that the judge declares a mistrial. It's not over till it's over, so don't let down your guard just because you think the decision is out of your hands.

During the deliberations, the jury may have questions about the jury instructions or the content of the testimony. They ask those questions by sending written notes to the judge with the assistance of the bailiff. Judges are wary of tainting the jury's decision through these communications and are usually cautious in their replies to the questions. Sometimes, after consultation with the lawyers, the judge may respond with a note instructing the jury to make a decision based upon the evidence before them. At other times, the judge may call the jury back into the courtroom and ask the court reporter to read aloud the portion of the testimony that pertains to the question. This question and answer process can become frustrating for the judge and the lawyers as well as for the jurors, but it must be handled with care in order to avoid a mistrial.

When the jury reaches a verdict, they notify the judge through the bailiff. The judge then summons the parties and lawyers to the courtroom. Once the parties and lawyers are present, the judge enters, and the drama begins. We've all seen it on TV — the part where the bailiff commands, "All rise," and everyone stands as a solemn jury files into the courtroom. Once the jury is seated, the judge, participants, and public take their seats as well. The camera pans around the courtroom, pausing briefly on members of the defendant's family, who anxiously await the jury's decision. The judge asks the presiding juror if the jury has reached a verdict. The presiding juror stands and answers, "We have, Your Honor," and hands the verdict sheet to the bailiff. The bailiff delivers the folded paper to the judge without opening it. The judge ceremoniously unfolds the document, reads it, hands it back to the bailiff, and the bailiff reads aloud, "We, the jury, find the defendant not guilty of all counts alleged in the indictment."[9] A sigh of relief issues from the crowd and is followed by smiles, tears, and embraces. The victorious defense lawyer congratulates the defendant and says a few final words of wisdom to those around him. The judge thanks the jury for their service and dismisses them.

The parts of a typical trial are presented above for your information and orientation. The terminology, order, procedure, and roles played by courtroom personnel may be somewhat different in your jurisdiction, but the basic concepts are uniform. At trial your lawyer should explain to the jury what the evidence will show, present your version of the facts, cross-examine your opponent's version, and point out to the jury what the evidence proved or failed to prove. The details may vary, but in every instance the lawyer orchestrates the case as a composer would an opera, portraying your story in the most compelling, persuasive, and believable terms possible.

3. Courts

Judges are charged with a duty to mete out justice according to rules and standards set forth in the law. Most dictionaries define justice as some combination of just conduct, fair dealing, rightness, fairness, correctness, or lawfulness. But justice is difficult to attain through the blind application of fixed rules. Unless flexibility is allowed, those rules can transform rather rapidly into harsh, inflexible edicts that seem to bypass justice entirely.

---

9. This practice varies greatly from court to court. Some judges read the verdict sheet aloud themselves, others pass it to the bailiff, court reporter, or presiding juror to be read.

Theoretically, the judge has the power to administer your case fairly and render a just verdict. It is possible, however, that you will neither be judged fairly nor receive a just verdict in your specific case. In fact, quite the opposite may occur. Judges are human and are invested with more power than some of them are capable of handling. That power can work for or against you when you appear before them. Problems with judges include ineptitude, egotism, favoritism, nepotism, corruption, and more. Any of these factors may affect your case.

3.1 Federal court

From the defendant's perspective, federal criminal cases are extraordinarily difficult to win no matter what the truth of the defendant's guilt or innocence may be. The cards are heavily stacked against the defendant in a federal criminal prosecution. The defendant's lawyer is at an extreme procedural disadvantage at every stage. Accomplished criminal-defense lawyers are often powerless to alter their clients' destinies even slightly.[10] Following are a few of the myriad problems that confront a defense lawyer in the federal criminal justice system:

- The same pool of jurors is used repeatedly during an extended period of jury duty. Federal prosecutors have multiple opportunities to hammer their opinions and attitudes into the jurors' heads during that time. After a while, the jurors become conditioned to convicting defendants. Each defense lawyer, however, sees the jurors only once.

- The questions asked during jury selection in federal court are delivered entirely by the judge.[11] Your lawyer may submit questions for the judge to ask, but the judge usually disallows most of them, rarely permits follow-up questions, and asks the few questions that are allowed in such an inept manner that the information the lawyers receive through the answers is mostly worthless.

---

10. Many of the Assistant United States Attorneys who prosecute these cases have never tried a case from the defense side. They are largely unaware of the enormous advantage that the rules provide in their favor.

11. In state court, your lawyer is allowed to question the jury panel directly.

- The education, training, and salaries of federal agents, investigators, and officers are generally superior to those of their state counterparts. The evidence they prepare for the United States Attorneys who take the cases to court is carefully cured of irregularities and is difficult for defense lawyers to penetrate. Federal agents are excellent at closing gaps in the evidence and smoothing over inconsistencies.

- Federal agents are given strong incentives to generate convictions. Promotions, raises, and other benefits are often linked, either explicitly or tacitly, to the number of convictions they obtain. Obtaining convictions is also a mark of prestige among their peers. With time, many agents lose perspective. Concepts like fairness and justice frequently take on secondary importance. The result is that many agents stretch facts to obtain convictions.[12] This insidious desire to obtain convictions is an ever-present evil with which all seasoned criminal-defense lawyers are familiar.

- Federal sentencing guidelines give federal judges little flexibility with respect to sentencing in criminal matters. Once the jury finds the accused guilty, the judge sets a date for sentencing and orders a presentencing report. Based on that report and a point system that takes into account a variety of factors, the judge then sentences the defendant according to strict guidelines set by law. Most of the defense lawyer's arguments are for naught.

3.2 State court

In state criminal cases, defense lawyers can do much more to defend their clients than in federal court. State court judges extend some courtesies to criminal-defense lawyers,[13] and state law usually allows more flexibility in sentencing. Making deals with the prosecution on the client's behalf and befriending the probation officers who make the presentencing reports are part of the game. When you appear in court and your lawyer seems to be

---

12. This happens in state court as well, but state and local police officers are not so well trained, so their attempts to bend the facts are often more transparent and easier to counter than in federal court.

13. In jurisdictions where judges are elected, lawyers' campaign contributions give them some leverage for obtaining dismissals, probation, and reduced sentences, especially when the offense is not against persons.

good buddies with everyone, don't worry. That's your lawyer's way of dealing with the system, and it can bring excellent results.

It may not be possible, however, to work out a deal with the prosecutor. Sometimes the defense must force the prosecution to present its case to a jury. Although most criminal defendants who go on trial are found guilty, in state court the defendant whose case presents marginal circumstances or mitigating facts has a fighting chance for acquittal. The end result, when the sentence is handed down, is often surprisingly fair. Unfairness in the state criminal justice system rears its ugly head more commonly in the early stages of the process. Mistaken identification, exaggerating the allegations against the accused (referred to as "over-indictment" or "over-charging"), and unnecessarily rough treatment by police officers are some of the problems that lawyers are frequently able to ferret out and redress. Thus the end result is often reasonable, but irreparable damage may have been done in the meantime.

Once I was appointed in state court to defend a little old man named John Smith[14] who had been arrested a couple of months previously and charged with a felony offense. A warrant had been issued for the arrest of one John Smith, and the police had arrested the first person with that name whom they ran across. There were 16 John Smiths listed in the city telephone book, and that did not include adult children living at home and persons without telephones!

I immediately filed a writ of *habeas corpus*,[15] attended a short hearing, and the judge ordered my client released. Mr. Smith was delighted to be free, and I was happy that I could help him. But how can he ever recover the two months of his life that he lost while sitting in jail? Justice ruled the day and the judge released an innocent man from wrongful incarceration. In the meantime, though, irreversible damage had been done to Mr. Smith's life. Unfortunately, this case is not exceptional. If you talk to criminal-defense lawyers in any state, you will find that each one has personal knowledge of cases that demonstrate similar injustices.

---

14. I have changed the name as a courtesy to the gentleman whom I defended.

15. A writ of *habeas corpus* is an order requiring that a detained person be brought before a court to decide the legality of the detention.

3.3 Bailiff

The bailiff is an officer of the court employed to maintain order in the courtroom. Bailiffs frequently talk to jurors and become friendly with some of them as the trial progresses. The bailiff's job is rather lacking in glamour, and courthouse gossip often becomes a specialty.

Be polite and friendly, but do not talk about your case around the bailiff. Comments made to the jury by any member of the judge's staff can dramatically affect the outcome of your case. Even though the judge admonishes the jury to talk to no one about the case, jurors may not understand that the admonition includes the bailiff. One simple word or facial expression from the bailiff as the jury files into the jury room can make or break your case. If you see or hear about such activity during the trial, tell your lawyer. You can decide together whether or not to report the incident to the judge.

3.4 Litigation can kill you

Most of us can cite a few key moments in our lives when we have felt threatened, weak, or helpless. Foremost among such moments would certainly be the death of a loved one or dear friend. Second to that would probably be a severe personal illness or illness of someone close to you. In third place might be a lawsuit, divorce, or other legal conflict. Legal problems, no matter how serious, pale before severe illness and death, but anyone who has been directly involved in a lawsuit will agree that most of the rest of life's problems seem minor when compared to the stress and strain of litigation. While a party to a lawsuit may be under great pressure and in no frame of mind to make sound decisions, that person's lawyer has a different perspective and can look at the problem objectively. Having a good lawyer reduces the stress of litigation and makes life livable while your lawsuit is pending.

The first few days after filing a lawsuit as a plaintiff or after being served with one as a defendant are particularly stressful. The minds of the worried litigants race at all hours of the day and night as they constantly review the facts, the strengths and weaknesses of their positions, and the law as they understand it. An aggressive plaintiff focuses on cornering the defendant into settlement or payment after judgment. A concerned defendant scrambles to construct a viable defense and to devise an alternative plan to protect hard-earned assets from execution of judgment should the plaintiff win.

Both plaintiff and defendant experience extreme mental and emotional fatigue throughout the litigation. The anxiety a defendant feels after being served with a lawsuit and before retaining a lawyer is severe. Such feelings diminish considerably after consulting with a lawyer and signing an attorney-client agreement. The reduction of stress is greater still if the lawyer is a good one. Some lawyers have a calming effect on their clients that is salutary, and once they are involved, the case proceeds in a smooth and rational fashion.

Stress is especially intense in disputes between family members, friends, neighbors, or partners in business. For all parties to lawsuits, though, stress levels are unbelievably high, and it is a wise and healthful move to retain competent legal counsel as soon as possible after making the decision to engage in a legal conflict. Doing so will reduce the tension considerably.

Another related problem is that with the exception of the plaintiff's lawyer in contingency cases, lawyers have little or no incentive to dispose of cases rapidly or efficiently. Rather, the opposite is true. Most of the incentives tend to make lawyers draw out their cases. Some lawyers rationalize this by claiming that the case must mature. As it matures, however, you, the client, are beset with anxiety while your lawyer calmly attends to other matters.

To achieve the result you seek, some maturation of your case may be desirable. In a situation where you have suffered a physical injury, for instance, it may be necessary to wait for the injury to completely manifest itself or for the medical work to be completed and billed before making a settlement demand.

In most legal battles, the parties start out ready to fight, with jaws set, stubbornly entrenched in their respective points of view. With time, however, they tire and become more realistic about their positions and the outcome. If a case is destined to settle, it will do so when the parties' attitudes have thus tempered. Some lawyers are able to bring their clients to that point much more rapidly than others. The ability to convince a client to take a rational stance is one of the hallmarks of a good lawyer.

Your best interest is served by being realistic about your case. Legal disputes are emotional affairs, and such emotion can severely impair your decision-making ability. Pride, idealism, ego, anger, fear, resentment, hatred, and all the other feelings that accompany being a litigant can bring disappointment, heartache, ulcers, or worse. Rarely does pursuing a case emotionally or out of principle pay off.

Listen to your lawyer. You are paying for legal services, and one of those services is to help you face the reality of your situation. Your lawyer is trained, not just to present your case at trial if necessary, but also to assist you in thinking through your legal problem. Communicating with your lawyer will make your case go more favorably for you and will greatly reduce the wear and tear on your body, mind, family, friends, and pocket book.

PART III

FIRING YOUR LAWYER

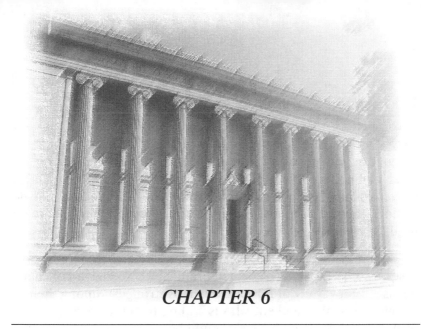

CHAPTER 6

MALPRACTICE

Lawyer malpractice is the failure on the part of a lawyer to use the knowledge, skill, and ability ordinarily possessed and exercised by lawyers, resulting in an actual loss to a client. It may arise out of the attorney-client relationship, or it may be based on a contract theory of liability derived from the attorney-client agreement. You can sue your lawyer for damages resulting from malpractice, and you may recover a monetary amount equal to the harm that you have suffered from it.

You cannot, however, sue your lawyer for a failure to meet ethical standards. A separate procedure exists to address ethical concerns, and it does not result in the recovery of your loss. Rather, the grievance process is designed to protect society by imposing sanctions that can include revocation of your lawyer's license to practice law. Legal malpractice and an ethical violation may exist under the same set of circumstances, but you should understand the difference and know that the remedies available to you are distinct for each. Ethical problems are discussed in Chapter 7.

1. Hiring a Malpractice Lawyer

If you believe that some action or inaction on the part of your lawyer has caused you to lose your case or has diminished the amount of your recovery, you may decide to sue your lawyer for legal malpractice. Such a decision will require you to find a lawyer to handle your malpractice lawsuit, and you should go through the same six-step process laid out in Chapter 1 that you used to select your first lawyer.

You may discover, however, that lawyers are hesitant to take cases against other lawyers. This reluctance to sue a colleague persists for a variety of reasons. Perhaps strongest among them is an awareness that a client who is willing to sue a former lawyer for legal malpractice obviously would be willing to sue a new one, too. Or perhaps the new lawyer finds a bit imposing the idea of suing someone who understands the workings of the law and knows how to supervise a tough defense. Most lawyers, though, simply do not want a reputation in the legal community for capitalizing on the misfortunes of their colleagues. For whatever reason, it may be difficult to find a lawyer who will take your legal malpractice case, even if it is meritorious.

If no lawyers in your locality profess to handle legal malpractice matters, take a look at lawyers who have experience in the medical malpractice area. Medical malpractice lawyers are acquainted with the performance standards required of professionals and the proof required to make a case against one. With a little luck, one of them will be willing to adapt that knowledge to your legal malpractice situation.

Yet another approach is to search in a neighboring county for a lawyer willing to take your case. A lawyer who does not want a reputation at home for feeding on colleagues' mistakes may welcome the opportunity to take a good case in another locality.

An additional challenge inherent in legal malpractice cases is finding lawyers to testify as expert witnesses. Lawyers are sometimes reluctant to testify against one another, so your new lawyer may find it difficult to convince a credible lawyer to appear as an expert on your behalf. If your lawyer perseveres, however, and your case has merit, eventually another lawyer will agree to give the necessary testimony.

You should be aware that there is a statute of limitations[1] on any possible malpractice claim that you may have against your lawyer. That statutory period begins with the commission or omission of the act alleged to be malpractice or when you first discover it, whichever comes later. Thus, it would be possible for the time to run out on your malpractice claim while your underlying lawsuit is still pending, if the case takes a long time and you knew about the lawyer's error.

Suing your lawyer can be a formidable task. Legal malpractice matters are complicated, and the defendant (your former lawyer) is familiar with the legal system. If you are thinking about representing yourself in a malpractice case against your lawyer, forget it. If you do, you will almost certainly lose. Your lawyer knows the ropes and is likely to have the sympathies of the judge, clerks, secretaries, bailiff, and nearly everyone else in the courthouse. Representing yourself would put you at an extreme disadvantage even if you have an exceptionally strong claim.

2. Proving Your Malpractice Case

Malpractice law is based on precedents established in court decisions rather than on statutes, and it varies according to fluctuating attitudes about the level of responsibility that the community believes professionals should have. Your malpractice lawyer must look to these decisions for the causes of action that are available in your state.

The two most common causes of action brought by clients against their lawyers are breach of contract and negligence. Of course, other legal theories may be used separately or in combination with these, such as fraud and theft.

To prove breach of contract you must show —

1) that an attorney-client relationship existed;

2) that the relationship was defined by a written or oral contract between you and your lawyer;

---

1. The statute of limitations is the period of time within which an action must be brought.

3) that your lawyer breached one or more of the provisions of the contract;

4) that the breach caused you injury; and

5) that your loss can be measured in money.

To prove negligence you must show —

1) that an attorney-client relationship existed;

2) that your lawyer owed you a duty of ordinary care in the handling of your legal matter;

3) that your lawyer failed to act as a lawyer of ordinary skill, knowledge, and diligence should have;

4) that the failure (negligence) caused your damages; and

5) that you suffered an actual loss or damages, usually measured in money.

Proving legal malpractice under a negligence theory is complicated because you have to show that your former lawyer was negligent *and* that you would have won the underlying case in the absence of that negligence.

An example of negligence would be if your lawyer missed the deadline for filing your lawsuit. A bad decision by your lawyer at trial regarding whether or not to call a witness or ask a specific question, however, would not necessarily constitute negligence. Trial lawyers make lots of decisions in the heat of battle that seem later to have been poor ones. Examined in light of the information that was available at the time it was made, though, the decision may appear reasonable.

A lawyer I know once represented the defendant against a plaintiff who was suing for injuries as a result of an automobile accident. The plaintiff was demanding a lot of money for the injury she had suffered, and he suspected that she was not being candid about the extent of her pain and suffering.

The first day of her testimony, the lawyer asked her several times if she had any diseases or illnesses, and she said that she did not. That evening, the lawyer's investigator obtained a medical record that showed she had syphilis, and the lawyer debated the wisdom of offering the record into evidence. Her testimony had not gone well for him, so he decided to introduce the document, not for the purpose of showing that she had syphilis (he didn't care about that), but rather to show that she had lied under oath. His hope was to discredit her statements regarding the extent of her pain and suffering. He knew the move was a risky one, but he opted to make it anyway.

Well, when he handed her the medical record and asked her about it, the woman began to cry, and when she could finally talk she sobbed that she had congenital syphilis and that she had been too ashamed to mention it before. Was the lawyer ever sorry he asked that question! He looked like an ogre for bringing up something that the woman could not help and that was not relevant to any issue in the case other than that of her credibility. He succeeded in making the point that she had lied under oath, but the question backfired on him. He had taken one step forward and two steps backward.

His decision to introduce the medical record turned out to be one that he regretted making, but it was not malpractice; it was simply one of many tough decisions to take calculated risks that are made during trial. He made a tactical move that actually strengthened the plaintiff's case. In the end, the jury awarded the plaintiff a goodly sum, although still less than the amount that had been offered before trial, but one cannot help wondering what the outcome might have been had that medical record not been introduced into evidence.

Legal malpractice involves monetary damages and is distinct from an ethical violation, which does not. An action or inaction by your lawyer may give rise to a legal malpractice claim, a grievance for violating the rules of professional conduct, or both. One does not imply the other. The filing of a malpractice claim will not get your lawyer disbarred. The filing of a grievance for an ethical violation will not preserve your right to file a lawsuit for legal malpractice. If you become involved in the grievance process, you may want to have a different lawyer examine the malpractice possibilities so that you do not inadvertently allow the time limit on a potential malpractice action to expire.

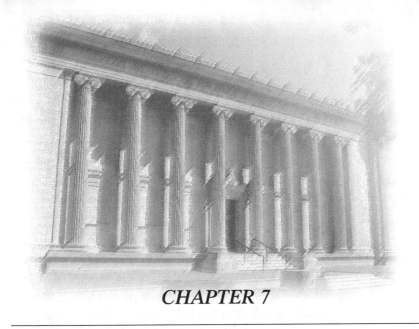

CHAPTER 7

LEGAL ETHICS

If your lawyer fails to observe a specific rule of professional responsibility that is imposed upon the legal profession by the state, you may file an ethic's complaint with the official body that monitors lawyers' conduct.[1] Each state has adopted rules of professional conduct or codes of professional responsibility that set minimum standards for the behavior of lawyers. Most states have modified the American Bar Association's model rules in some fashion and use names like Missouri Rules of Professional Conduct or Virginia Code of Professional Responsibility. To insure a complete understanding of the rules by their licensed lawyers, many states require that their bar applicants pass a professional responsibility exam as a requirement for admission.

The procedures for processing grievances are similar among the states. A special staff initially reviews the complaint and either dismisses it or sends it on for further investigation. If the complaint appears to have substance, a panel of hearing officers, usually comprised of three persons, holds a formal hearing. The

---

1. Names for these bodies (committees) are almost as numerous as the states themselves. They include Grievance Committee, Disciplinary Committee, Department of Lawyer Regulation, Office of Bar Counsel, Board of Professional Ethics and Conduct, Office of the Disciplinary Administrator, Board of Bar Overseers, Attorney Grievance Commission, Professional Conduct Committee, and more.

lawyer's action must be proved to have constituted misconduct by "clear and convincing" evidence.[2] After the hearing, the panel makes a disciplinary recommendation to the state's highest court.

When you have a conflict with your lawyer, you must identify its nature before you can know what to do about it. The problems that can occur vary widely. I list only a few examples below:

- Your lawyer, in an action in which you are one of several defendants, does not seem to be giving your case the attention that you think it deserves. You discover that your lawyer has received instructions from the insurance company (which is paying the legal fees for all of the defendants) to take it easy on the billing and allow one of the other defense lawyers to take the initiative. You have a right to your lawyer's diligent attention to your case, and if you do not receive it, you may file a grievance with the ethics committee.

- Your lawyer steals money from you. This can happen in various ways, from the lawyer's commingling of personal funds with your funds to refusing to return the unused portion of a deposit or retainer. You can file a grievance or sue your lawyer for conversion or fraud. Every state now has a special fund, provided by the lawyers themselves, for the protection of clients. The funds usually cover theft, fraud, and embezzlement, but not negligence.

- Your lawyer sexually harasses you. Should your lawyer sexually harass you or request sexual favors, even in the most subtle of ways, you should file a grievance and look for another lawyer.

The road to disciplining a lawyer for transgressions is a long and rocky one. In addition, at the end of that road, you receive no compensation. Five types of discipline are normally available:

a) *Private Reprimand (or Informal Admonition)*: This amounts to a scolding by the state bar organization — a slap on the wrist — and it is done without publication. In most jurisdictions, this information is public record (you can obtain it) even though it is not published.

---

2. In a few jurisdictions, the standard is a "preponderance" of the evidence.

b) *Public Reprimand (or Published Censure)*: This is a written reprimand from the state's highest court that sets out the details of the violation and is published in the state's bar journal or other state publications.

c) *Probation*: The state's highest court imposes special conditions on the lawyer's practice that are tailored to the lawyer's specific problem. In some states, diversion programs are available; if the lawyer resolves the problem, the complaint is dismissed and the record remains confidential.

d) *Suspension*: The state suspends the lawyer's license for a specified period of time or indefinitely.

e) *Disbarment*: Disbarment removes the lawyer from the practice of law for a minimum period, with the only opportunity for readmission being through a formal hearing.

1. Firing Your Lawyer

Any time after you enter into the attorney-client agreement, during trial or on appeal, you have a right to fire your lawyer and hire a new one. Of course, your lawyer may become upset, threaten you with all kinds of unpleasant things, demand immediate payment of expenses and fees, or refuse to turn your file over to you, but you still have a right to change lawyers whenever you so desire. You should, however, exercise extreme caution in doing so in order to avoid jeopardizing your case and your finances. If your case is in an advanced stage, it may be more prudent to continue with your original lawyer than switch.

Once you decide to change lawyers, you have several options. You can go to your lawyer's office and announce that you intend to seek new counsel, or you can telephone your lawyer or write a letter to communicate your desire in a less confrontational fashion. No matter how you decide to effect the dismissal, you should write a letter to your lawyer confirming your decision and requesting the prompt delivery of your file to you. Some clients send friends or family members to pick up the file and are surprised when the lawyer refuses to release it. No one can retrieve your file for you, and no lawyer will deliver it to a third party. You can, however, authorize retrieval by your new lawyer. Otherwise, you must take custody of the file yourself.

Many criminal defense lawyers will not talk to a client who is currently represented by another lawyer, so in such a situation you may have to dismiss your lawyer before contacting a new one. If you are a defendant in a criminal matter and you paid a fixed fee to the first lawyer, you will still have to pay a fee to the second lawyer before that lawyer will accept your case. Your previous lawyer will probably not return your money, so changing lawyers may mean that you will have to pay twice.

In civil cases with contingency-fee provisions, you may also end up paying more than you bargained for. A client's separation from a lawyer can be a messy affair, and some lawyers refuse to get involved until the dust has settled and the split is complete. Before taking your case, the new lawyer may wish to understand the extent of your prior lawyer's claim to attorneys' fees. Your former lawyer may file a lien or sue you to preserve fees that will be taken out of a future jury verdict or settlement. No lawyer who has spent months working on a case will stand idly by while another lawyer collects the fee. The two lawyers may be able to work out an equitable division of the contingency fee, and the total cost to you may be no greater than what you initially contracted to pay. You may also have to pay the expenses that your lawyer has accrued on your behalf at the time you retrieve your file.

After you dismiss your first lawyer, your new lawyer will prepare the appropriate substitution documents for the court and help you retrieve the parts of your file that are necessary to continue your case. Under no circumstance can your former lawyer withhold documents vital to your ongoing case. You have a right to change lawyers and take your documents with you.[3]

2. Confidences and Secrets

Your lawyer has no right to give away confidences that you have revealed in the course of the attorney-client relationship. Documents that you turn over to your lawyer may contain information that the rules of professional conduct require be protected. Even

---

3. Once a case is over, a lawyer may be permitted to retain a file pending the payment of attorneys' fees and expenses. In no event can a lawyer withhold documents that are necessary for a case that is in progress.

a subpoena[4] for documents held at your lawyer's office may not be enough to justify giving away a secret or a confidence. If a judge orders the production of specific documents containing secrets or confidences, the lawyer does not violate the duty owed to you by revealing just that information.

If your lawyer releases information or documents that you feel are confidential, you should obtain an opinion as to the propriety of that action from one of the members of the state grievance committee. The committee member you talk to will not charge you for the conversation, and your inquiry may be the first step in an investigative process that protects not only you but also others.

Although your lawyer has an ethical duty to safeguard your confidences, in some limited situations your lawyer may legitimately reveal them. This occurs when the safety of others or the integrity of the court is involved. Should you, for example, tell your lawyer that you intend to harm a witness in your case, your lawyer, if your threat seems real and you appear to be capable of carrying it out, may be permitted to reveal your intention to the judge.

In the same way, your lawyer may be allowed to reveal a confidence should you indicate an intention to lie under oath.[5] This problem becomes, at times, a subtle game between the lawyer and the client. Most lawyers are not about to blow a good case by telling the judge that the client intends to lie under oath. If the client lies and is caught, the lawyer simply feigns ignorance and surprise. Usually such lies become so obvious in the crossfire of the questioning at trial that it is unnecessary for the lawyer to clarify that the client misrepresented the facts, although in civil cases it would seem to be the lawyer's strict ethical duty to do so.

Another exception to the rule that a lawyer must safeguard a client's confidences occurs in situations in which the client files a grievance or malpractice action against the lawyer. In such an event, the client waives any privilege of confidentiality, and the

4. A subpoena is a written order that commands a person to appear in court. Special subpoenas can also require the production of books, papers, business records, or other documents to be used in courtroom proceedings.

5. In some criminal-defense situations, a lawyer may be prohibited from revealing a confidence even with knowledge that the accused intends to lie under oath.

lawyer is free to tell the entire story and construct a defense without restraint.

In the criminal-law context, I have observed several situations in which the defense lawyer revealed the defendant's intention to harm an accuser or witness. In each of those cases, the judge chose to ignore the threat on the theory that once the prosecution ended, the defendant's anger would subside and no one would be hurt. Indeed, nothing bad happened to anyone in those instances, but I can assure you that the defense lawyers and the judges were distressed by the decisions they were required to make before the trials began.

Once I was sitting in court waiting for a hearing, and another lawyer was waiting with his client for a jury to enter the courtroom to announce its finding after deliberations. The jury came out, declared the defendant guilty, and was dismissed. To the surprise of everyone present, as the jury was filing out of the courtroom, the defendant's mother stood up in the area where the public was seated and shouted that she was going to kill the judge! The judge calmly looked at his court reporter and asked, "Do you have that on record?" The reporter responded, "Yes, Judge." Then the judge said, "Ma'am, I am sending you to jail. Bailiff, place this woman under arrest."

The woman was taken to jail, and when she was finally released, she did not attempt to harm the judge. Judges know that most threats are uttered under stress and that when the moment passes usually nothing comes of it.

3. Diligent Representation

A lawyer cannot simply decide that a case is not so meritorious as it seemed at first and then ignore it. I know of one instance in which a lawyer allowed an associate to accept a number of cases of marginal merit so that she could gain trial experience. Soon thereafter, the associate left the firm and refused to take the bad cases with her. Fortunately for the clients involved, the senior lawyer took the matters seriously and worked them to their conclusions, but he swore that he would never again allow an associate lawyer to take on a practice case.

I know of another lawyer whose associates decided to leave the firm all at the same time. Instead of farming their cases out to other lawyers, he ignored the matters of lesser value and worked on the ones he felt were likely to pay off. One of the ignored cases was dismissed because the lawyer did not respond to a motion filed by the defendant. The case was not a very good one and might have been dismissed in any event, but the lawyer owed a duty to the client to pursue the case diligently, and he failed to do so.

Your lawyer has a duty to represent you competently and diligently. Anything less is unacceptable. Your lawyer should get tough when it's appropriate, in spite of any personal relationship with the opposing lawyer. An experienced personal injury lawyer once told me, "I have yet to meet a good lawyer who does not step on anyone's toes." I agree with him. You hire a lawyer to step on toes, to fight hard for your cause. You have every right to expect hard-fought representation to the limits that the law and common sense allow.

PART IV

OTHER RELATED TOPICS

CHAPTER 8

ALTERNATIVE DISPUTE RESOLUTION

Alternative Dispute Resolution (ADR) is the popular general term for a number of alternatives to full-scale litigation. At the beginning of this chapter, I describe two common forms of ADR — arbitration and mediation. The chapter concludes with a section on small claims courts, which are also alternatives to the more formal courts.

1. Arbitration

Arbitration refers to the hearing of and decision on a dispute between two or more parties by an arbitrator. Normally, a sole arbitrator is selected by mutual agreement of the parties. In some instances, a panel of three arbitrators hears the case. If there are to be three arbitrators, each party selects one, and then those two agree on the third. Other selection methods may be employed as well.

Arbitration differs from mediation in that the arbitrator renders a decision after hearing the facts. In mediation, the mediator facilitates the reaching of an agreement by the parties and does not render a decision. This does not mean, however, that the arbitrator's ruling is always binding on the parties. If it is not binding, and either party is not satisfied with the result, the dissatisfied party can still present the matter to a regular court.

In court, the procedural rules afford the plaintiff and the defendant relatively equal chances of success; the rules do not noticeably lean one way or the other. Binding arbitration, however, is decidedly biased in favor of the defense. That is why so many of the form contracts that people sign have arbitration clauses. The lawyers who draft those contracts know that binding arbitration favors defendants. If their clients are companies selling products or offering services that would make them, in the event of litigation, more likely to be defendants than plaintiffs, the lawyers include a clause requiring binding arbitration. The explanation given to the individual who must sign the contract is that arbitration is a fast and painless way to resolve disputes, everyone is doing it nowadays, and the company's form contract cannot be altered. Most people sign, simply because it is too much trouble to object and they do not expect to have a problem anyway. When a conflict surfaces and they consult a lawyer, they are dismayed to find that the first thing the lawyer wants to do is try to defeat the arbitration clause in the contract and pursue the matter in a regular court. Most lawyers know that prosecuting a plaintiff's case in a binding-arbitration proceeding is an uphill battle.

Some experts claim that arbitration costs less than courtroom litigation. My experience, however, is that arbitration is often the more expensive option. When an individual initiates an action in court, the filing fee is modest, and the tribunal costs are free of charge to the litigants. Public courts are funded with tax dollars. The judge, courtroom, bailiff, court reporter, and jury are provided to the parties by the taxpayer with no additional charge to the individuals involved in the litigation.[1]

Not so with arbitration. The fees charged by the arbitrator and the arbitration organization can be thousands of dollars. The filing fee for the arbitration tribunal is often based on a percentage of the amount in controversy, and the arbitrators' hourly billing rates are comparable to those of practicing lawyers.

---

1. In some jurisdictions, the litigants must pay a jury fee, but it is nominal.

The procedural rules in our public court system evolved over time to meet the needs of the parties. Litigation typically requires —

a) a physical place for hearings, meetings, and the trial;

b) a presiding officer, trained in the law, to rule on legal questions both before and during the trial;

c) a mechanism for exchanging information and obtaining testimony in advance of the trial so that the parties may properly prepare their presentations;

d) a means of enforcing the orders of the presiding officer so that the parties do not withhold information, delay the proceedings, or otherwise frustrate the purpose of the tribunal;

e) a method of keeping a record of the proceedings so that adverse rulings and judgments may be appealed; and

f) an appellate body to correct errors committed at the trial level to the detriment of one party or the other.

The parties' needs are constant no matter what kind of tribunal is selected. And if those needs are the same, the costs to fulfill those needs will inevitably be similar. The cost of a deposition, for example, is the same whether taken for use in court or arbitration. Expert witnesses charge the same amount per hour for testimony in either forum. Lawyers' fees will also be roughly the same; your lawyer must do approximately the same amount of work in either forum.

Arbitration can be more expensive than going to court, however, because the parties have to foot the bill for the arbitration tribunal.

Imagine yourself as the plaintiff in an arbitration proceeding and paying tribunal fees, arbitrator's fees, attorneys' fees, deposition fees, expert-witness fees, and other expenses. The opposition returns your interrogatories with a series of evasive answers, and when you ask for sanctions, you find that the sanctions at the arbitrator's disposal have few teeth in them and that the arbitrator is little disposed to use them. When plaintiffs run into such obstacles in arbitration proceedings, they often settle their cases, and these settlements, unfortunately, are negotiated from positions of weakness rather than strength, so the results may be unsatisfactory.

The judge in a public court, however, can impose sanctions or hold the parties or their lawyers in contempt of court. Parties and lawyers who refuse to comply with court orders can be fined or even jailed. In many jurisdictions, the judge can also dismiss the plaintiff's case or render judgment against the defendant as a sanction. Arbitrators also have the power to dismiss cases or render judgment against dilatory defendants, but they have none of those other scary powers that make lawyers so wary.

Most people entangled in litigation care about the outcome. They want to win. It makes no sense to go to war with clubs and spears (arbitration) when you can use missiles and bombs (court). The procedures available in the public court system, when followed by skillful lawyers and fair judges, expose all the facts, facilitate the application of the correct law, and make justice possible.

Situations do exist, however, where arbitration may be an advantageous alternative to the public court system. It is particularly effective for labor-contract negotiations and trade disputes in which the commodity or business is one requiring detailed market or product knowledge.

2. Mediation

Mediation is a method by which the parties can try to work out their own solution to their conflict under the supervision of a neutral third person. It is becoming increasingly institutionalized as an option to which judges turn before hearing a case. In many jurisdictions, judges require that the parties attempt mediation before being heard in court.

Mediation has become a popular means for judges to reduce their caseloads. Divorce and personal injury cases are commonly sent to mediation as a first step in resolving the conflict. Mediation has become a marvelous tool for finding common ground between disputants and capitalizing on it to help them settle their differences. The mediator supervises a dialogue wherein the parties themselves reach a mutually agreeable settlement, and the parties are expected to carry out the agreement in good faith.

The mediator opens the sessions by meeting with both parties together in a room. The setting is informal; normally, the mediator sits at the head of a table and the parties take positions on either side, facing one another. If the hostility between the participants is especially strong, the mediator may rearrange the seating or may meet with the parties separately to try to neutralize some of the hard feelings.

The mediator begins with an explanation of the ground rules for the mediation. The parties must conduct themselves in a civilized manner; allow one another to speak without interrupting; and refrain from the use of foul language, gestures, threats, or other inappropriate behavior. The mediator asks the plaintiff to review the facts, and then the defendant is allowed to speak. These initial statements are often emotional and rarely conciliatory. The mediator asks questions of either side to clarify what was said and further break the ice between the parties. Skillful mediators are often able to elicit answers that find areas of potential compromise that the parties had not thought existed.

In many instances, though, the friction between the parties is such that the mediator must meet with each one separately to try to work through the obstacles and come up with a suggested approach to settlement. Sometimes the mediator must go back and forth between the parties several times before reaching a solution. If everyone remains engaged in the mediation process, though, usually a solution will be forthcoming.

The result of the mediation, if all goes well, is a written agreement between the parties. It is not binding, so nothing compels either side to comply with its terms. In practice, however, compliance with mediation agreements is high. Most people want to put their bad experiences behind them and will live up to the agreement. The agreement is signed by the parties, the mediator, and when a court is involved, the judge. The underlying lawsuit is dismissed when the terms of the agreement have been executed.

Mediation will not get you that slam-dunk win you may have dreamed about; you can accomplish that only in a court of law. Most situations do not merit such clear victories, however, and in cases where the parties have ongoing relationships, mediation offers an excellent alternative to the expense, pain, and stress of going to court.

3. Small Claims Court

Small claims courts deal with civil (noncriminal) matters in which the amount in controversy is less than a stated maximum amount, ranging from $1,000 in some jurisdictions to $15,000 in others. For the most part, small claims courts employ rules that are simpler than those applicable to other state courts, and there is a high tolerance for laypersons (nonlawyers) who are using the system for the first time. Usually, though not always, the parties must represent themselves, and no lawyers are allowed to appear in the case. In all instances, the parties are free to be coached by lawyers outside the courtroom; and in a few states, lawyers are allowed to appear on behalf of their clients.

If you have questions concerning the operation of the small claims court in your jurisdiction, you should ask the court clerk for help. The court clerk will not, however, advise you on the legal aspects of your claim. The assistance you receive will be procedural, such as how to fill out the complaint,[2] arrange for service of process,[3] and obtain the issuance of subpoenas. When you file your claim, you will receive an information brochure explaining the procedures of the court. The brochure is not part of the paperwork served on the defendant, so a defendant must obtain it by calling the court clerk's office and requesting that it be mailed or by going to the clerk's office to obtain it. The information may also be obtained on the Internet by running a search using the name of your state and the words "small claims court."

When you calculate, before filing suit, the dollar amount that reflects your damage or injury, and you find it to be greater than the maximum amount allowed in the small claims courts in your

---

2. The name of the document used to initiate the action varies from state to state to include complaint, petition for relief, plaintiff's statement, and statement of claim.

3. Service of process is the delivery of the notice to the defendant that the plaintiff has filed a lawsuit.

state, you have two choices. You may proceed in small claims court and be satisfied with the maximum recovery allowed, or you may sue in a higher court for the full amount. For example, if your damages are $6,000, and the small claims court's jurisdictional limit is $5,000, then before going to a higher court, you must decide if it's worth retaining a lawyer and incurring the higher filing fee in order to recover the $1,000 difference. It may make sense to choose the small claims court even though the recovery is limited, because of the low cost, speed, and convenience of that forum. Once you make this decision, however, there is no going back. You will have waived any further claim to the difference.

Small claims courts are intended primarily for cases that can be measured in dollar amounts. In many states, the small claims court judge can render judgment only in terms of money. In other states, however, the judge can find the equitable (nonmonetary) solution and order the parties to comply with it. If you want the judge to award something other than cash, you should ask the court clerk if that possibility exists in your jurisdiction before including that request in your complaint.

One advantage to filing in small claims court is that the filing fees are less than those of higher courts and are sometimes set on a sliding scale, depending upon the amount of money you seek in your complaint. States increase the amounts of their filing fees from time to time, so it's difficult to state the range accurately, but the fees are reasonable. You can learn the amount from the court clerk, the court's information brochure, or the Internet.

Before you go to trial in small claims court, you must prepare your case. This preparation is important because it may help you settle the matter, and it will increase your likelihood of success at trial.

As a first step, you should contact the opposing party by telephone, state your reason for calling, make a settlement demand, and set a deadline for the response. Do not get angry, make threats, or argue your position. Anything you say can become evidence against you, and you may be asked about the conversation at trial. If you are easily angered or tend to talk too much, you should contact the other party only in writing. You can damage your case by saying too much, so limit your conversation to the basic facts, settlement demand, and deadline. Do not worry if your phone conversation does not bring positive results. Your testimony at trial will be that you attempted to resolve the problem directly with your adversary and that your attempt failed.

If your deadline brings no resolution of the matter, send a letter (Certified with Return Receipt Requested) restating the problem, making your demand, and setting a deadline for your opponent's response. Do not be argumentative, and do not threaten legal action at this time. Anger is natural when you feel you have been cheated, injured, or otherwise wronged, but displaying it is a surefire way to lose. The party who is the most level-headed and reasonable frequently wins the close decisions.

If the deadline passes, and you do not receive the response that you seek, send a second letter, again Certified with Return Receipt Requested, but this time indicate that if you do not receive satisfaction within a prescribed period of time, you will take further action.[4] Be sure to refer to your first letter and any reply. You should keep copies of all letters, receipts for certified mail, and proofs of delivery. You will need them at trial.

Before you sue in small claims court, you should answer several important questions:

a) *Does your case fall within the statutory amount for small claims court?* You can file your claim in small claims court if the amount in dispute is less than the dollar limit set for that court in your state.

b) *Does your case involve a cause of action that is excluded from small claims court?* Certain causes of action cannot be pursued in small claims court even though the amount in controversy is within the court's jurisdictional limit. The court clerk can give you information regarding what is excluded. If you think your case may be excluded, you should talk to a lawyer to ensure that your assessment is

---

4. One might use the term "legal action" here, but it is probably best not to do so. Your correspondence will become evidence in your case, and threats to sue do not help you look like the good guy.

correct and to determine whether the case merits treatment in a higher court. You should not make this judgment yourself.

c) *In what locality within your state should you file the action?* Normally, you should initiate the action in the jurisdiction where the defendant resides or where the breach or injury occurred.

d) *When should you file the action?* You must file your claim within the time limit set by the statute of limitations. If you do not file before the time runs out, you forego your opportunity to do so.

e) *Do the rules allow a lawyer to appear for you?* One problem with small claims court, ironically, is that the claims are small. If you are not extremely careful in your use of a lawyer there, you may find yourself spending more money on legal fees than your case merits. In most cases, however, it's advisable to consult with a lawyer for a half hour or so to get some general guidance as to how to proceed. If you go into the lawyer's office prepared with questions, you should have no trouble obtaining all the guidance you need at a relatively low cost.

f) *What are the procedures for service of process on the opposing party?* The court clerk will provide you with information regarding this requirement.

g) *What evidence should you present at trial?* You should be prepared to present all of the evidence that favors your case. You should familiarize yourself with the order of trial beforehand. Basically, each party has an opportunity to make an opening statement, present evidence, and deliver a closing argument. (See Chapter 5 for a more complete explanation of the order of the trial. Most small claims courts do not allow juries, so ignore the parts that deal with jury trials. The remaining elements of the trial are substantially the same but are greatly simplified in small claims court.)

On the day of trial, you present yourself in the courtroom and wait for the judge to call your case. In many small claims courts, the judge asks before calling the first case which of the parties present in the courtroom would be willing to attempt mediation. The willing candidates raise their hands and are assigned to mediators who are present for that purpose. If you reach a settlement through the mediation, you sign a written agreement and your case remains on file until its terms have been executed. If you do not agree to mediation, or you fail to reach a settlement in the mediation session, your trial will be heard that day.

When your case is called, go forward and take a seat at one of the tables in front of the judge's bench. You should have with you the documents that you plan to use in your presentation and the questions that you plan to ask of your witnesses. Once you and your opponent have taken your places, the judge will ask the plaintiff to explain the problem. Then the defendant will be allowed to speak. The trial is semiformal, so the judge may ask questions during and after the opening statements to clarify the facts as the parties relate them.

Once the judge has a basic understanding of the controversy, the parties are asked to present their evidence. The categories of evidence you can typically present are as follows:

a) *Your own testimony.* Legally, your testimony alone may be sufficient to make your case, but it's advisable to present supporting evidence as well. If your verbal statements fulfill all of the legal elements of your case, the judge can rule in your favor based solely on your testimony, so do not give up hope just because you have no other evidence. Be sure to talk about the defendant's liability, the amount of loss you have suffered, and your costs in taking the action to court. Your costs include the filing fee, the fee for service of process, long-distance telephone charges, photocopy charges, postage, and any other expenses that you incur.

b) *Factual witnesses.* Factual witnesses are people with direct knowledge of something that happened related to your cause of action. You can use them to establish an element of your claim of which you have no direct knowledge, to bolster your own testimony, or to corroborate facts that you anticipate the opposition will contradict.

c) *Documentary evidence.* This includes letters, photographs, receipts, contracts, rental agreements, and any other documents that you feel will support your position in the case. Do not forget to offer your demand letters into evidence. Photocopies of documents are usually allowed, but you should check with the court clerk beforehand to see what form of documentary evidence is admissible.

d) *Expert witnesses.* Most expert witnesses are too expensive to use in small claims court, but you may find exceptional circumstances that justify such expense or an expert witness who is willing to testify for no charge or for a modest fee.

After both you and your opponent have presented your evidence, you will have an opportunity to make your final arguments. You should keep your remarks brief and to the point; a minute or two will probably be sufficient. Sometimes saying nothing at all is best. The judge knows the law and has listened to the evidence, so making an extensive argument may be counter-productive.

The judge will, in the majority of cases, render a judgment on the spot. Should you not agree with that judgment, do not display anger or any negative emotion. If you feel that the result is unfair or not in accordance with the law or the evidence, you may want to appeal. An appeal is not available in all states, so you will have to inquire as to whether or not one is permissible in yours. Some states allow only the defendant to appeal, some allow both parties to appeal, and some allow neither to do so. In order to appeal, you must learn the time limit for filing, how to file, and the type of proceeding that is generated by the appeal. In some jurisdictions, an appeal will mean that you do the entire trial again before a higher trial court. In other jurisdictions, your appeal will generate a review of how the judge applied the law. This can be difficult, because usually no stenographic record is made at small claims court proceedings. Thus, there may be nothing for an appellate court to review.

You should remember several things at trial in small claims court:

a) *Be organized.* Do not waste the court's time on extraneous matters. If you limit your presentation to relevant information, you greatly increase your chances of success. It helps to make notes in advance of the trial of what you want to say at each stage.

b) *Dress well and maintain a respectful demeanor.* You should dress well for court and look as neat and well-groomed as possible. Always stand and face the judge when you are talking. If your opponent addresses you directly, listen without interrupting and then turn to the judge and ask if you should respond. Speak only to the judge and do not initiate any conversation with your opponent once the trial has begun.

c) *Do not act like a lawyer.* The small claims court is an inexpensive forum for laypersons to present their respective sides of a controversy in plain English in a semiformal setting. Be polite to everyone, especially the judge, and present your evidence in your own words. The judge knows you are not a lawyer and will appreciate your not being pretentious.

d) *Be calm and reasonable.* Being calm and reasonable in your dealings with the judge, staff, and opposing party will bring you success faster than any other approach.

e) *Do not sign a release or dismissal until you have received payment.* If the defendant agrees to settle the case before the trial, you should not sign a release or dismiss your lawsuit until you have received payment according to your settlement agreement. Collecting that money will be far easier and more certain if the suit remains hanging over the defendant's head. If the offer to settle takes place in the courtroom on the day of the trial, explain to the judge that a settlement offer has been made and request that the trial be rescheduled for a later date. If the defendant pays before that date, you dismiss the lawsuit. If not, you proceed to trial.

CONCLUSION

I wrote this book because I saw a need for a straightforward explanation of how to engage the services of a lawyer. I presumed there to be folks like me who when faced with legal problems want to know enough about the process to make wise decisions. Most readers who have come this far and have finished this book are of that ilk. If you are part of that group, you are to be congratulated. You have made an important move toward taking charge of your destiny.

You now know the basics of how to select, work with, and fire a lawyer. In addition, the insight you have gained into the way lawyers work will make you more at ease as your case progresses, allowing you to sleep peacefully at night rather than tossing and turning in bed with angst. You can recognize when your lawyer is artificially inflating legal fees or improperly preparing for trial, and you have a feel for the other difficulties that can befall those who do not pay close attention to their lawyers' activities.

Even with this knowledge and insight, however, you may find it difficult to avoid conflicts with your lawyer. I don't pretend to have a magical formula for the perfect attorney-client relationship, but I can say with confidence that informing yourself about the way lawyers operate is the first step toward achieving that end. Some of you who read this book will escape the perils that lurk in your path — your lawyers will work diligently, your cases will go smoothly, and you will live happily ever after. Inevitably, though, some of you will be besieged by misfortune and will perceive your lawyers as having whipsawed you in spite of your efforts to understand the process. In all probability, your experience will fall somewhere between those two extremes, and the information you glean from these pages will help minimize your lawyer troubles and the impact they have on the outcome of your case.

As you learn to work with your lawyer, you will feel yourself gaining the positive energy you need to be successful. You may suffer setbacks from time to time, but if you continue to strive with your lawyer toward a common goal, you will overcome the obstacles in your path. You can obtain excellent results from the use of a lawyer, but to do so you must become involved in your case. If you persevere, you will be richly rewarded for your efforts.